INTRODUCTION TO COMPUTERS AND PROGRAMMING

INTRODUCTION TO COMPUTERS AND PROGRAMMING

JESSICA HELLWIG

Columbia University Press
New York and London
1969

Jessica Hellwig is a member of the staff of the
Columbia University Computer Center.

Copyright © 1965, 1969 Columbia University Press
Library of Congress Card Number: 71-85919
Printed in the United States of America

Cover photograph of circuitry, courtesy of IBM

for

KIT

in gratitude

PREFACE

This book and its earlier versions have been used continuously at Columbia University since 1965, in an introductory course offered by the Computer Center to students, faculty, and members of the University research staff. The text was developed to fill a very specific need: to give to academic research workers a strong conceptual foundation in the general principles of automatic computation, in order that they might, if they so desired, learn a programming language easily by taking an intensive course or by studying a manual.

It is more correct to say that the introductory course offered by the Columbia University Computer Center *is* this text. It was intended as a self-study book, and has been used successfully as such; the Center's first course has neither lectures nor an instructor. The text has also been used, however, in the first part of the first semester of graduate and undergraduate computer science courses at the University.

The objective of this book is not to teach programming, but to provide an introduction to the basic characteristics of computer systems and of the programming activity. It is intended to serve a dual purpose. For students and research workers who need to learn how to program, it attempts to provide a foundation that will allow them to make sense of the often apparently arbitrary conventions of computer technology. For readers who do not become actively engaged in programming, it attempts to provide enough understanding that they can interpret or supervise the work of others, as well as attempting to satisfy some of their curiosity.

The analogy between computer programming and driving a car is an old favorite; dissatisfaction with this analogy is central to the spirit of the text. To be sure, many drivers know nothing about the way a car is put together, or about the basic principles of the internal-combustion engine. Many of these people, furthermore, are excellent drivers. They tend to be rather helpless, however, when anything goes wrong with the car; and they are rather at the mercy of the garage mechanic (to say nothing of the automobile salesman). One of the purposes of this text is to leave the research worker less to the mercy of the computer consultant.

During the prime of the second generation of computers, hopes were high that the third generation would give rise to operating systems that would make computers more accessible to the amateur programmer. The opposite proved to be the case, and we have found at Columbia that the third generation demands much more understanding of the nature of operating systems on the part of even our most dilettante users. Thus, although I had originally expected to reduce the discussion of operating systems from what appeared in the original version of the text, I have instead felt it necessary to expand it. I do not regard this as a positive evil, however; nor am I certain that, were the available systems close to transparent, I would refrain from attempting to expose them.

Although the objective of the text is to develop an understanding of general principles, the method used is to present specific illustrations of these principles. In particular, the FORTRAN language, the IBM 360 computers, and variants of the IBM operating system known as OS/360 are used as exemplars of many of the subjects that are covered.

The orientation of the examples is definitely toward scientific applications, although little mathematical sophistication is assumed. Readers who were not utterly terrified by high school mathematics should encounter little difficulty in following the arguments set forth here.

The number of exercises is relatively small, and varies considerably from one chapter to another. Some of the subjects covered -- notably the representation of information discussed in Chapter 3 -- are profitably augmented by practice. The material in Chapters 4 and 5, on the other hand, is discursive and exploratory, and not conducive to concrete, practical tests of comprehension. Essay questions may be appropriate here for classroom use; these, I feel, should be left to the pleasure of the instructor.

Chapters 2, 4, and 6 include phases of a central major exercise, the development and submission of two FORTRAN programs for computer processing. Many of the concepts discussed in the text are illustrated by these programs. The final exercises of Chapter 6 build on the experience acquired by running the programs; they pose fairly difficult questions, and can be used to generate discussion and further questions in a classroom environment.

Few writers can ever have owed so much as I do to three people: to Kenneth M. King, without whose support I could have neither begun nor finished; to Robert R. Fenichel, who encouraged me with the first version, and who is the most gratifying reader and painstaking critic imaginable; and to Stefanie Tashjian, who taught me most of what I will ever come to know about writing. Needless to say, my failings are not theirs.

I owe grateful acknowledgment of aid and comfort to the entire staff of the Columbia University Computer Center, every one of whom has helped me in this undertaking. I am especially indebted to Peter Graham, Linda Pirasteh, Betsy Schoch, and Joyce Kerr, who provided patient and constructive comment. Susan Leeds and Juana Diaz-Marta worked hard and imaginatively on the manuscript. Above all, unnumbered thanks go to the many members of the Columbia University community who have been our students and readers in past years, and who not only endured and responded, but often had the courage to come back for more.

Finally, I must apologize to the august company of oceanographers for the liberties I've taken with their discipline.

Jessica Hellwig
March 1969

CONTENTS

CHAPTER 1. BASIC COMPUTER CONCEPTS
  1. Introduction   1
  2. Organization of a Desk Calculator   2
  3. Organization of a Digital Computer   4
  4. Computer Units   5
  5. Programs, Flow of Control, and Flow Diagrams   7
  6. Types of Computer Instructions   15
  7. Instruction Codes and Programming Languages   24
  8. Programs in Memory; Subprograms   27

CHAPTER 2. STEPS IN COMPUTER PROBLEM-SOLVING
  1. Statement of the Problem   31
  2. Analysis of the Problem   33
  3. Computational Procedure   35
  4. Flow Diagram   37
  5. Coding the Program   40

CHAPTER 3. INFORMATION STORAGE AND PROCESSING
  1. Memory Structure: Terminology   48
  2. The Central Processing Unit   49
  3. Differentiation of Instruction and Data   53
  4. Core Storage and Data   54
  5. Positional Number Systems   61
  6. The Binary Number System   68
  7. Hardware vis-a-vis Software   73
  8. Binary Representation of Real Numbers   75
  9. Binary Representation of Alphabetic Characters   78
  10. Binary Instruction Code and Related Topics   82

CHAPTER 4. THE COMMUNICATION OF INFORMATION
  1. Input and Output of Information   87
  2. Information-Storage Media: Printing and Punched Cards   91
  3. Information-Storage Media: Magnetic Tape   103
  4. Information-Storage Media: High-Speed Large-Capacity Devices   107
  5. Input/Output Devices for People   109

CHAPTER 5. OPERATING SYSTEMS
- 1. Programming Systems and Operating Systems Distinguished ... 120
- 2. Classic Batch-Processing ... 121
- 3. I/O Channels and Interrupts; a Chronicle of Wasted Time ... 128
- 4. Multiprogramming Systems ... 132
- 5. System Evolution: Multiprocessor Systems ... 134
- 6. Time-Slicing ... 143
- 7. Time-Sharing or Interactive Systems ... 146

CHAPTER 6. FURTHER STEPS IN COMPUTER PROBLEM-SOLVING
- 1. Punched Output ... 158
- 2. The Printed Listing ... 160
- 3. Checking the Results ... 176
- 4. System Diagnostics: Compiler Messages ... 179
- 5. System Diagnostics: Linkage Editor and Library Messages ... 184
- 6. A Final Illustration ... 189
- 7. Conclusion ... 194

APPENDIX I. THE IBM MODEL 029 KEYPUNCH ... 195

APPENDIX II. ANSWERS TO EXERCISES ... 199

INDEX ... 211

INTRODUCTION TO COMPUTERS AND PROGRAMMING

CHAPTER 1

BASIC COMPUTER CONCEPTS

1. *Introduction*

    This text is the nucleus of a course that introduces the nature and use of electronic digital computers. Whether the text is incorporated into such a course or read independently, it will familiarize the reader with some concepts basic to automatic computing as it exists today. These concepts should be grasped thoroughly before an attempt is made to learn the specific techniques of computer usage.

    Learning to use a computer has been likened to learning to drive a car, in that one may master the techniques without knowing anything about the internal organization of the machine. To a great extent this is true, but such an approach, if taken at the extreme, requires that rules be presented in an arbitrary and ritualistic light, and that the learning process be reduced unnecessarily to rote. Comprehension of the general principles of computer organization is all that is needed to make the techniques meaningful.

    The word *computer* can refer to any member of a broad class of computational devices, including the abacus, the slide rule, and so forth. In this course we shall concern ourselves exclusively with electronic digital computers, and when we refer to 'a computer', it is one of this type that we shall mean. More particularly, we shall in many passages describe a specific machine, the IBM 360, as well as certain auxiliary IBM equipment. Even more particularly, we shall occasionally describe the computing facility of the Columbia University Computer Center.

    Reference to these particulars, however, is not intended to restrict the scope of the text. Descriptions of hypothetical machines at hypothetical computer centers lack salt as well as precision, and where illustrations are helpful, specific ones are more so. The reader should find little difficulty in identifying instances of parochial usage, and the text will help him, from time to time, to make appropriate generalizations.

On the other hand, the student should bear in mind that the computing field is young and burgeoning; that an amazing diversity is one of its principal characteristics today; and that, as with any young field, truly sturdy generalizations are hard to come by. This text makes no attempt to offer such generalizations, and it might be said of almost every statement herein: "Yes, but there's another way that can be done, too." In a sense, the whole course is a concrete illustration of typical but by no means universal computing practices. Students who 'get their feet wet' in this course, and who then go on to experience the real diversity of the real world, will be in a position to help in formulating those generalizations that the field requires.

2. *Organization of a Desk Calculator*

Let us begin by considering the organization of a standard desk calculator. The calculator performs arithmetic operations upon data values that are entered by means of a keyboard; the sequence of operations is controlled by another set of keys, such as an add key, a multiply key, and a shift key; the results of operations are displayed in a set of dials, or they may be printed on a strip of paper. There are four distinct functions involved: *arithmetic* operations; entering of data values (called the *input* function); *control* of the sequence of

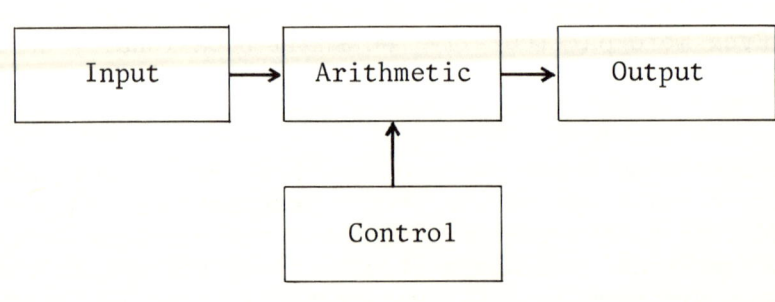

Figure 1.1

operations; and display of results (called the *output* function). There are four calculator components, or *units*, corresponding to these functions, as represented in Figure 1.1.

The input unit provides a facility for entering data values into the calculator.

The control unit provides a facility for specifying operations to be carried out on the input values.

The arithmetic unit provides the means whereby the specified operations are carried out.

The output unit provides a facility for displaying the results of the specified operations.

Now suppose we are using a desk calculator to compute the value of

$$d = (e + s)/2$$

for ten pairs of values for *e* and *s*, which are written down in a table as follows:

e	s	d
100	9000	
99	8950	
51	9127	

etc.

The process of computing the ten values of d will consist of the following actions on the part of a human operator:

1. clear the calculator by hitting the 'clear' key;
2. enter the value of *e* via the keyboard;
3. hit the '+' button to add it in (adding it to zero);
4. enter the value of *s*;
5. add *s* to *e* by hitting '+'; record the sum as an intermediate value;
6. clear the keyboard and enter the intermediate sum by

use of the 'divide entry' button;
9. read the result from the output display unit and enter it into the table under d;
10. repeat steps 1 through 9 for all remaining pairs e and s.

The word *program* is defined in the dictionary as 'a plan of procedure.' Steps 1 through 10 in the preceding example may be described as a desk calculator program.

3. *Organization of a Digital Computer*

It would be possible to develop a desk calculator with very high-speed electronic circuitry, capable, for example, of performing a single addition in a few millionths of a second. This would be of little practical value, however, because the time it takes to solve a problem on the calculator is almost completely limited by the speed of the human operator of a manual keyboard; the operator cannot enter the data or control the operations at anything remotely approaching such speeds.

In addition to the slowness of manual input and control, the desk calculator method of computation is extremely tedious, since we must repeat exactly the same steps over and over. What we require for efficient computation includes the following:

(a) the ability to specify, once only, the sequence of operations that must be performed, and to have them repeated automatically as desired;
(b) the ability to present all the input data at once, and to have the appropriate data items chosen automatically when they are required;
(c) the ability to have the automatic operations, implied in (a) and (b), performed at very high speeds *and* with very high accuracy.

We can accomplish the first two of these goals, in fact, in a very simple manner. We employ an assistant, a person who knows how to follow instructions and read data accurately. We present him with a clearly labeled tabulation of the data.

Then we go away and wait for the answers. This is a tolerable mode of operation, but we have not gained any speed, and we cannot be sure of the accuracy of our results.

A digital computer is designed to satisfy all of the requirements outlined above, and in addition to reduce repetitive human labor. Like a desk calculator, the computer performs arithmetic transformations on input data. Like the calculator, it must have an *input unit*, an *output unit*, an *arithmetic unit*, and a *control unit*. The control unit of the computer, however, embraces the functions of both the calculator's control unit and the human calculator operator, as we shall see presently. And in addition to these units, the computer has a memory, or *storage unit* (Figure 1.2).

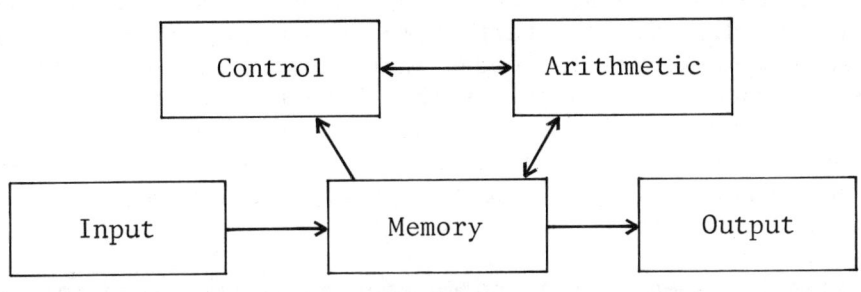

Figure 1.2

4. *Computer Units*

The memory of a computer is simply a large bank of electronic circuitry capable of storing information. The information is stored in a very general way, and it may represent almost anything you like, as we will see later. In particular, we can store numbers in the memory, such as the table of values for e and s in the desk-calculator problem. Whatever information is stored in the memory can be retrieved selectively whenever it is needed. Therefore we can satisfy condition (b) above; we use the input unit to enter our data into the memory, and we can 'read out' of memory, when necessary, any piece of data.

The arithmetic unit is capable of performing elementary arithmetic operations, and it receives orders from the control unit. The control unit, however, is not operated manually, as is that of a desk calculator. The control unit will interpret and cause the execution of an entire sequence of arithmetic operations, and repeatedly, as many times as required for solution of a problem. The sequence of operations need be specified only once, so that our first condition (p. 4) has been satisfied: "the ability to specify, once only, the sequence of operations that must be performed, and to have them repeated automatically as desired."

This automatic control is accomplished, in the computer, by storing the program of instructions, as well as the data, in memory. A set of arithmetic operations, similar to those described for solving $d = (e + s)/2$, may be put into a special code and stored in a section of the memory. The control unit may then be directed to start at the beginning of this section of memory and execute the coded instructions sequentially, operating upon the data values that have been stored in another section of memory. The set of instructions (called a *program*) will be repeated until, for example, there are no more data. Alternatively, it is possible to specify exactly how many times it should be repeated.

Also included in the stored program may be coded instructions for printing out the answers to the calculations via the output unit.

Observe, now, that once a program of instructions has been outlined, the program and the data have been input to the memory, and the control unit has been instructed to begin execution, the solution of the problem is completely automatic; no more human intervention is required until the end, when the results are examined. Since the intermediate computational steps are performed by electronic circuitry, under automatic control, it is now possible to take advantage of the very high speeds attainable through electronic technology.

In addition, assuming that the instructions and the data have been properly recorded, we have eliminated human error from the system.

5. *Programs, Flow of Control, and Flow Diagrams*

It may be concluded from the previous discussion that there are three major advantages gained by using a computer, to wit: speed, accuracy, and the ability to describe, once only, a procedure which is to be repeated many times. Indeed, once the procedure has been described (i.e., once the program has been written) two different kinds of repetition are possible. First, the program may include instructions for repeating certain sequences of operations, or subsections of the program, a desired number of times. Second, the entire program may be preserved, and at a later date it may be reintroduced into the memory unit, together with a new set of data, to be executed again.

Let us look more closely at what is meant by a computer program. A program explicitly specifies a procedure for carrying out a computation. A program consists of a set of instructions that the computer is capable of executing. If the program is stored in memory, the control unit may be directed to cause execution of each instruction in the specified sequence.

Normally the program instructions are executed in the order in which they are stored. This is called the 'normal flow of control.' Control (or the control unit) is initiated at, say, instruction number 1; after 1 is executed, control will automatically pass to 2, and so forth, where the instructions are physically stored in sequence.

The flow of control may be changed, however; certain instructions, which may also be included in the program, direct the control unit to transfer to a different location in memory rather than continuing in sequence. For example, consider a typical section of a program. The problem is the same as the one used in the discussion of the desk calculator: solve $d = (e + s)/2$ for many values of e and s.

1. Fetch a value of e from the data area of storage.
2. Add the corresponding value of s.
3. Divide the result by 2.
4. Store this result as the corresponding value of d.

The flow of control will be from 1 to 2 to 3 to 4. Now we want to repeat from step 1, so we indicate this by the next instruction:

    5. Transfer control to 1.

Instead of trying to find an instruction 6, the control unit will next select instruction 1 and then continue the normal flow; the sequence will be: 1,2,3,4,5,1,2,3,4,5,1,2....

Normally when we want to describe a program and also to indicate its flow of control, we do so by means of a diagram, rather than verbally as we did above. A *flow diagram* or *flow chart* of the solution of $d = (e + s)/2$ might look like Figure 1.3.

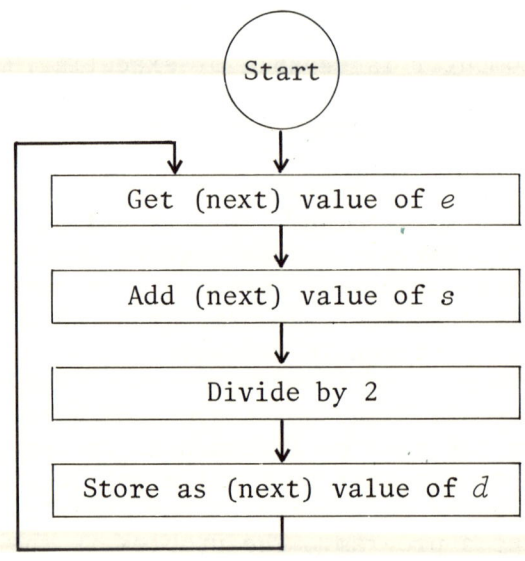

Figure 1.3

Flow diagrams are an indispensable part of the preparation of a computer program. There are many ways in which they can be drawn, and a variety of flow chart conventions exist. We will discuss them more thoroughly later on, but let us

8

observe a few important things here. The steps in the computation are described in boxes; a box may contain the description of a very simple computational step, or the summary description of a fairly complicated sequence of steps. For example, the flow diagram on the preceding page might also be as illustrated in Figure 1.4.

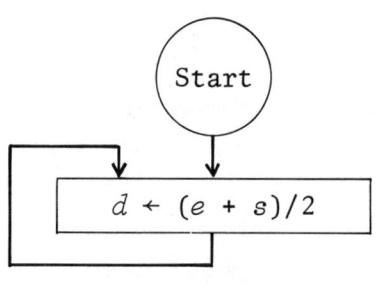

Figure 1.4

The lines with arrows indicate the flow of control. If several operations are combined in one box, as in the second diagram, then the flow of control is assumed to be *normal*, or sequential, between the instructions implicitly described in that box. In other words, any *transfer of control* must be explicitly indicated by the flow diagram.

The rectangle enclosing the formula in Figure 1.4 is referred to as a *compute box*. The expression $d \leftarrow (e + s)/2$ is an abbreviated way of saying: "Compute d, using the formula $(e + s)/2$," or "Evaluate the expression $(e + s)/2$ and set d equal to that value." The symbol '$\leftarrow$' is called the assignment symbol and indicates that whatever is to the left of the arrow is to be assigned the value of the expression to the right. An equals sign is often used instead of the left arrow:

$$d = (e + s)/2$$

But it is important to note that the equals sign has here exactly the same significance as the left arrow: in particular it does not signify mathematical identity.

That is, to write in a computer flow diagram

$$a = 10 \quad\quad \text{or} \quad\quad a \leftarrow 10$$

does not mean to assert that the value of the variable a is ten. Rather, it means: *make* the variable a have the value of 10. The distinction is clearer when we write

$$T = T + 1 \quad\quad (T \leftarrow T + 1)$$

which is unacceptable if the equals sign is interpreted in its ordinary mathematical sense. What this means as a computer operation -- in a flow diagram, for instance -- can be paraphrased thus: "Take the current value of T, add 1 to it, and make the result the new value of T." If we started with T equal to 77, the result of

$$T = T + 1$$

would be to give T the value 78.

EXERCISES

1.1   The sequence of numbers

$$3, 9, 27, 81, 243, \ldots$$

is a geometric series; each number in the series is three times the preceding number. In general, a geometric series has a base R, and each number in the series is R times the preceding number. The expressions

$$R, R^2, R^3, R^4, \ldots, R^n$$

are the first n terms of a geometric series with base R.

Suppose that we want to evaluate every term for some given value of R. If we set the first term equal to R, we can describe a general rule for obtaining each term in the series: each term is equal to R times the preceding term.

A step-by-step procedure may be given as follows; fill in the missing elements in steps 4 and 6:

1. Get the value of R (input data)
2. Store this as the value of the first term.
3. Take the value of the term just found.
4. _____
5. Store this as the value of the next term.
6. Transfer control to ___.

1.2   The sequence in which the instructions of Exercise 1.1 will be executed is:

$$1, \_, \_, \_, \_, \_, \_, \_, \_, \_, \_, \_, \text{etc.}$$

Check your answers at the back of the book before going on.

1.3 The following incomplete flow diagram corresponds to the procedure outlined in Exercise 1.2. Complete the diagram.

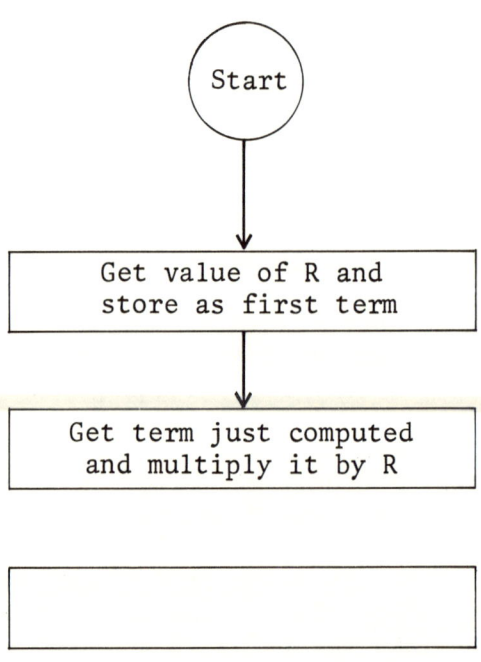

Check your answer before going on.

1.4 Suppose that besides computing each term of the geometric series we want to evaluate the sum of the terms

$$S = R + R^2 + R^3 + \ldots + R^n$$

and suppose furthermore that we are interested only in the value of the sum. That is, we compute each term only in order to add it to the sum. We could evaluate all the terms and store them in memory, just as we did above, and then add them

all up to arrive at S. On the other hand, since we don't need
to preserve the values of the terms, we can do something simpler.

Instead of saving every term, we can save only the latest one. Each new term is derived from the last by multiplying it by R. If we let the sum accumulate as we go, by adding in each new term as we calculate it, there's no need to save more than one term. Study the flow diagram below and then answer the questions.

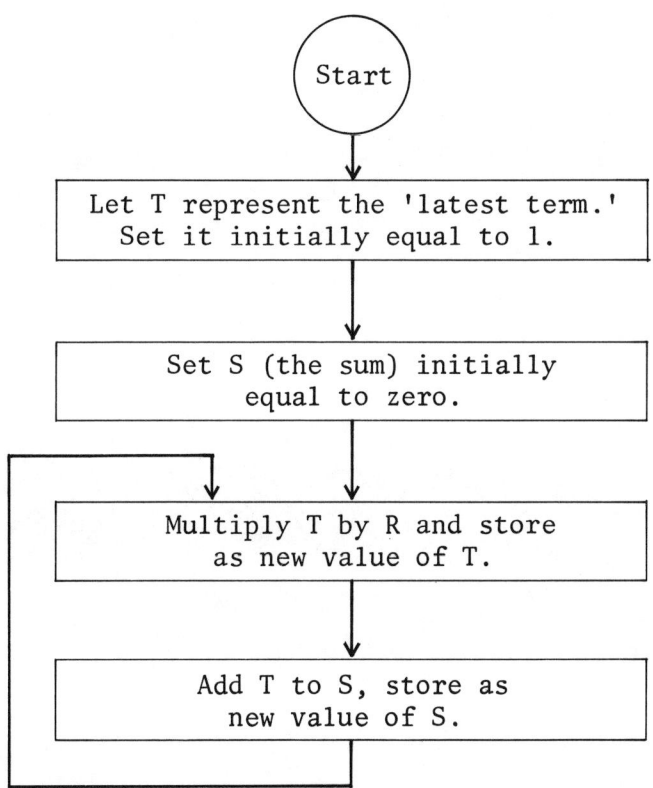

The variable T takes on many different values throughout the execution of this program. Assume that R = 1/2.

The first value assigned to T is ____.
The second value assigned to T is ____.

```
The third value assigned to T is ____.
The first value assigned to S is ____.
The second value assigned to S is ____.
The third value assigned to S is ____.
```

Check your answer before going on.

6. *Types of Computer Instructions*

The instructions that comprise a computer program are taken from a clearly defined set of operations that the computer is capable of performing. These operations fall into three types. One group of operations is *arithmetic* in nature, and includes addition, subtraction, multiplication, and division. In the flow diagram of a program it is not necessary to describe each arithmetic operation involved in each step of the computation. Where d is to be computed, for example, we simply write the formula, which indicates the required operations.

A second group of operations is available for *input* of data and *output* of results. Earlier we described the program as residing in one area of memory while the data reside in another. In most cases, the program includes instructions for introducing data into the memory from some external medium. The data may be introduced, or *read in*, at any point in the program. Similarly, data, including computed results, may be *written out* of memory onto some external medium by instructions included in the program. The data upon which a program operates may be input all at once, or they may be read in a little at a time, as needed by the program.

The flow diagram of Figure 1.4 must be extended to allow for input and output (Figure 1.5).

The third group of operations is associated with the flow of control. We have already encountered one such operation, called an *unconditional transfer*. It is indicated in Figure 1.5 by the arrow that loops back to the beginning. It is called unconditional because whenever the flow of control reaches the transfer instruction, control will always be routed to the part of the program that the transfer instruction specifies.

Also included in the group of control operations is a type of instruction called a *conditional transfer*. This type is what makes the whole idea of a prewritten, stored program workable. If you examine the flow diagram below (Figure 1.5), you will see that the flow of control is essentially a *loop*;

15

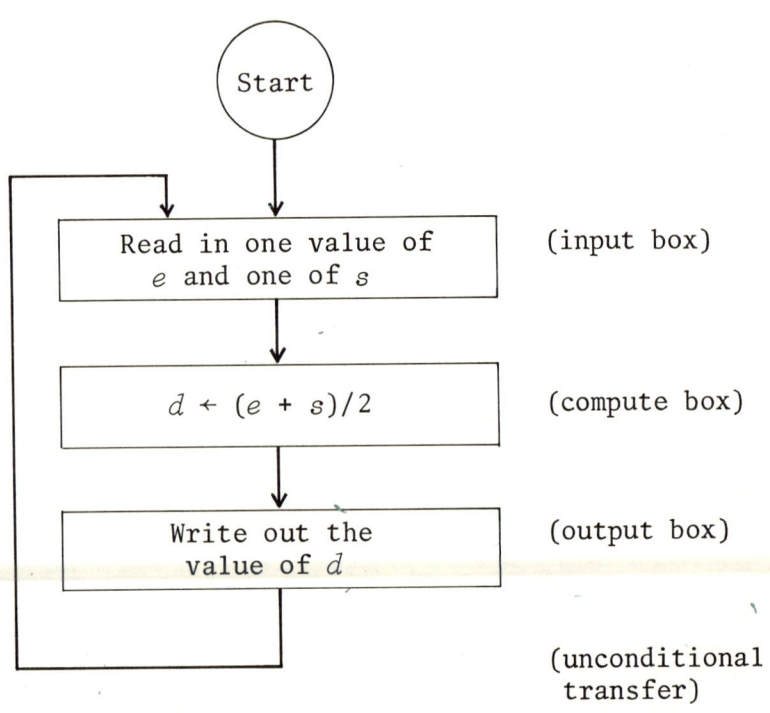

Figure 1.5

the instructions in the input, compute, and output boxes are executed repeatedly, and ad infinitum. There is nothing which will terminate the iteration of these instructions; this type of flow is referred to as an *infinite loop*, and it is a fundamental programming error. Conditional transfers are instructions that allow you to specify that a change in the control path (i.e., a *branch*) is to be effected if and only if a certain condition holds true. This may be indicated in the flow diagram by a special kind of box, called a *decision box* (as illustrated in Figure 1.6).

Conditional transfers require the computer to make *logical decisions*. A logical decision is simply a choice determined by the truth or falsity of a clearly verifiable condition. (The word 'logical' is used in a formal sense, where the required form is: If A is true, then do B. Hence the statement "If

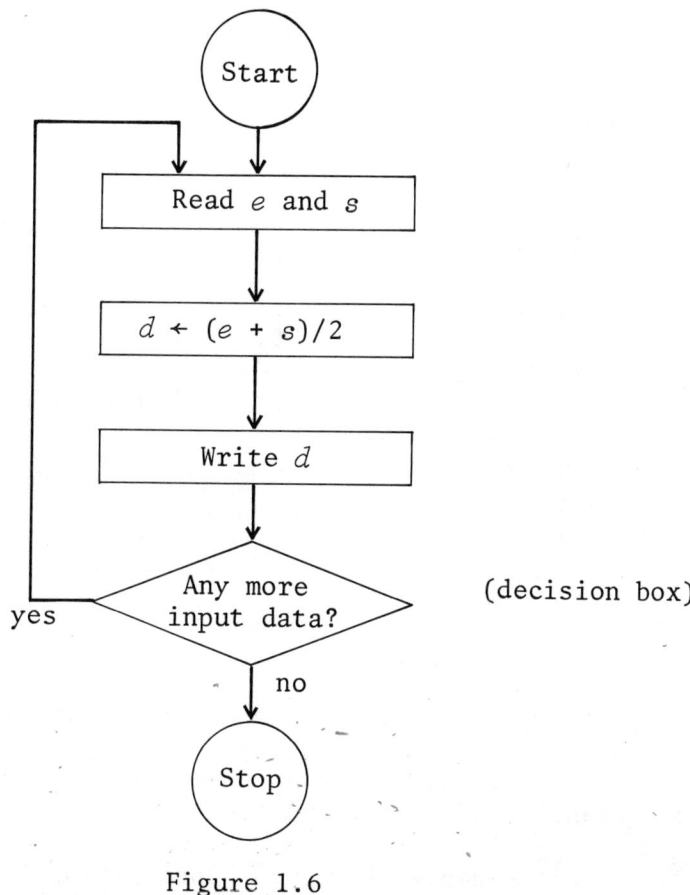

Figure 1.6

I'm wrong, I'll eat my hat" describes a logical decision, however illogical it may be in an intuitive or contextual sense.) The computer can make certain simple logical decisions of the form: If A is true, then transfer to instruction n (otherwise, continue the normal flow of control). One of the more common conditional transfers is called a 'transfer on minus'; "If (some quantity is) negative, transfer to instruction n." This may be diagrammed as in Figure 1.7.

In this section of a program, A is computed and then its value is tested. If A is negative, control follows a new path and B is evaluated as the square root of -A (a positive quan-

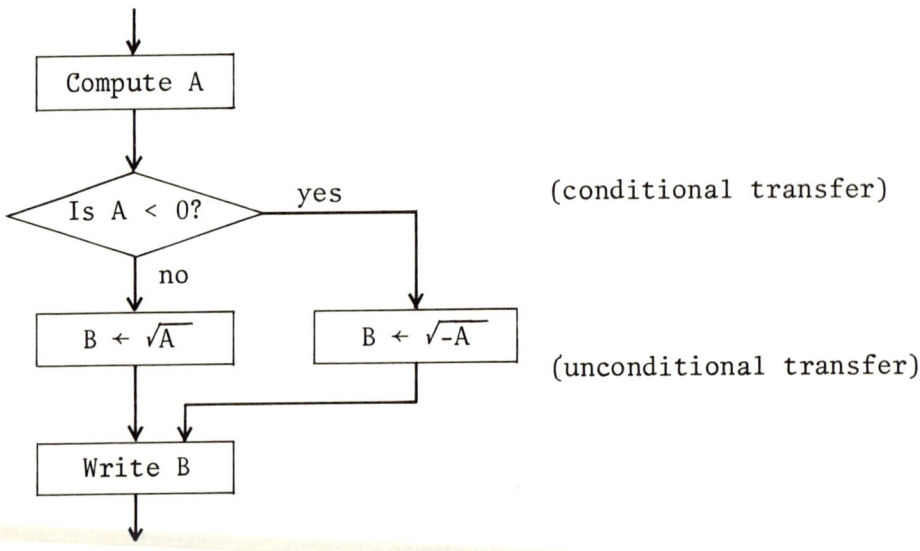

Figure 1.7

tity); if A is positive (or zero), B is set equal to the square root of A. After B is evaluated, on either branch, the flow of control is reunited (by an unconditional transfer on the 'Yes' branch) and the normal flow continues.

As this example shows, the unconditional transfer is sometimes necessary. It is responsible for the erroneous infinite loop of Figure 1.5, but that is because it has been misused, not because there's anything inherently incorrect about unconditional transfers.

EXERCISES

1.5 The following flow diagram was presented in Exercise 1.4. It needs some improvement.

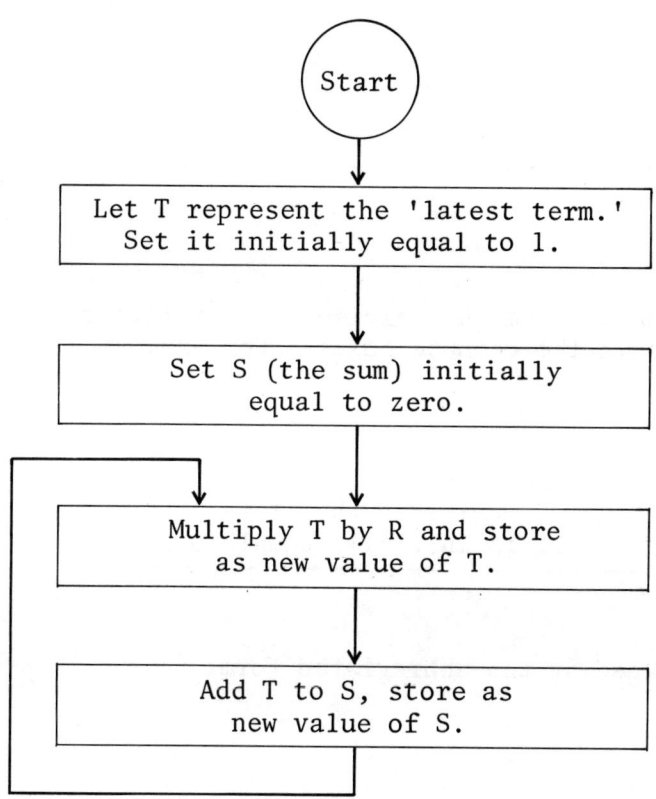

First, this diagram does not provide a means of establishing the value of R, the base of the geometric series. If we want to be able to use the program many times, for computing sums of geometric series with different bases, then the value of R should be input data. Fill in the description that should go inside an input box to be added to this diagram:

```
┌─────────────────────────────┐
│                             │
│                             │
└─────────────────────────────┘
```

1.6 The diagram in Exercise 1.5 has rather long-winded descriptions in the compute boxes. For example,

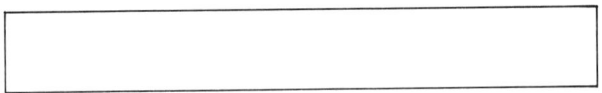

can be replaced by the abbreviated form:

```
┌─────────────────────────────┐
│            T ← 1            │
└─────────────────────────────┘
```

Remembering the significance of the left arrow, write the other three compute boxes of the diagram in abbreviated form.

Check your answers before going on.

1.7 Now rewrite the flow diagram for the geometric series problem, using abbreviated notation and inserting the input box. There are several possible places where the input box could go, and several where it must not go. Be careful. After drawing the diagram, mentally trace the flow of control, using several of the successive values assigned to the variables, before looking at the answer.

Check your answer before going on.

1.8 In the flow diagram of Figure 1.6 we use a decision box to determine whether to repeat the loop or to terminate the program. The question of when to terminate a loop is always an important one in programming.

Returning to the sum of the geometric series: How is the loop to be terminated? As the diagram stands now (as of Exercise 1.7) it is incomplete, as we have an infinite loop and no output. The output should be the sum, S, and it should be written out after all terms have been added into S. As the problem was originally stated, we were to sum the first n terms of the series, i.e.,

$$S = R + R^2 + \ldots + R^n$$

where n is some integer. The value of n might be given in the statement of the problem, which might read: "Sum the first 50 terms of the geometric series on R." On the other hand we might want to write a program that could be used over and over again for different values of n as well as different values of R. In that case we would not fix the value of n in the program itself, but let n be input data. The input box would be written as:

Read R, n

We will also need an output box of the form:

$$\boxed{\text{Write S}}$$

since S is the desired result. Before this can be inserted, however, we must find a way to terminate the compute loop after the nth term has been added to S.

For this purpose, we will introduce a *counter* which will be another variable. Let us define a variable I with an initial value of 1, and let us increase I by 1 every time we execute the loop. We will want I to be 1 when T is equal to R, I to be 2 when T is equal to R^2, and so forth. Then we can compare I with n every time, in order to decide whether to repeat the loop or not.

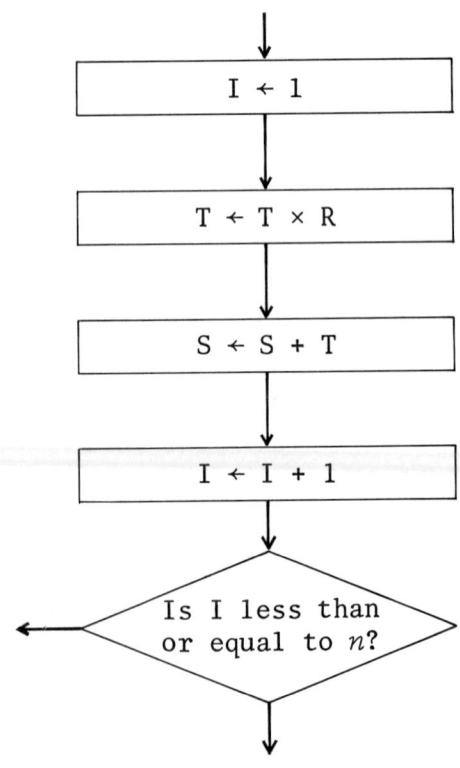

Complete this diagram, labeling the branches 'yes' and 'no' as in Figure 1.6, and showing where each branch leads. Combining this with the results of Exercise 1.7, produce a complete flow chart from 'Start' to 'Stop.'

Check your answers before going on.

7. *Instruction Codes and Programming Languages*

A program, then, is a set of computer instructions that perform input, output, arithmetic operations, logical decisions, and direction of the flow of control. A flow diagram indicates what instructions are required and in what order they must be written. On the basis of the flow diagram, one should be able to write the appropriate instructions. These are written, in practice, in any one of a variety of special *codes*, or *programming languages*, and the process of writing them is called *coding*.

The various languages used for encoding instructions differ in their degree of complexity and in the demands they make on the coder and on the computer itself. By way of a brief illustration, let us consider the compute box in the flow diagram discussed earlier,

$$d \leftarrow (e + s)/2$$

and the coded instructions necessary to describe this computational step.

The computer instructions for doing the arithmetic, and the data (values of e, s, d, and the number 2), must be stored in the memory of the computer in a form that can be detected by electronic circuitry. In many computers, the physical representation of the information consists of groups of magnetic polarizations; these can be imagined as groups of tiny switches capable of being turned on or off. As we will see in Chapter 3, appropriate groupings of switches can be used to represent very complex information.

In order to talk about the structure of the information in the machine, we can use a code to represent, more or less explicitly, what is stored in the memory at a particular time. The representation will be more or less explicit depending simply upon how explicit we need to be.

One kind of code represents an instruction as a string of letters and digits. If you know the code, which is sometimes called *internal machine language*, you can tell exactly what is in the machine. The code is usually different for different types of computers.

Here is an example of an instruction for the IBM 360, represented in an internal machine code:

$$7840F02A$$

This instruction can best be thought of as having several parts, and pictured like this:

$$78\ 4\ 0\ F02A$$

The first part, 78, is an *operation code*; the operation performed by this instruction is 'get from memory.' The rest of the instruction specifies what to get and where to put it. The second part, 4, identifies a special part of the arithmetic unit that is used for holding numbers, and is called 'register number 4.' The third part, 0, isn't used in this particular instruction. The fourth part, F02A, designates the location in memory of the data item that is wanted. The whole instruction can be paraphrased as: "Get from memory the number stored at location F02A and put it in register 4 (so I can use it for calculation)."

Coding the program for $d \leftarrow (e + s)/2$ in internal machine code would require that we assign memory locations to the data. We might make an assignment like this:

Location in Memory	*Data Value Stored There*
F02A	e
F02E	s
F032	d

The values of e and s will be stored at those locations before the calculation begins. The value of d will be stored at F032 after the calculation is completed. The program could now be coded thus:

Instruction	Paraphrase
78 4 0 F02A	Get the number at location F02A and put it in register 4 (e).
7A 4 0 F02E	Add to what's in register 4 the number at location F02E (s).
34 4 4	Divide what's in register 4 in half, and put the result in register 4.
70 4 0 F032	Store what's in register 4 into memory location F032 (d).

This internal machine code exactly represents the computer instructions. Programs are not written in this type of code, however (although they were some years ago). Because writing instructions in internal machine code is extremely tedious and error-prone, other codes have been devised which are simpler to use and which may be automatically decoded into machine instruction. These more usable codes are called programming languages. The trend of the development of these languages is toward describing computer programs in something approaching natural language. We will discuss this subject in more detail later on, and for the moment will merely illustrate the coding for $d \leftarrow (e + s)/2$ in two other forms.

Rather than writing instructions in their numeric form, we may write them in an alphabetic code which allows us to use mnemonic symbols to some degree. The language used here, called *symbolic machine language*, also relieves us of the necessity for assigning specific numeric addresses to data items as we had to do using internal machine code. The instructions given above have the following counterparts in symbolic machine language:

Symbolic Code		Paraphrase
LE	4,E	'Load' register 4 with the value of e.
AE	4,S	Add to it the value of s.
HER	4,4	Halve the sum in register 4.
STE	4,D	Store it as the value of d.

The codes LE, AE, etc., correspond to the portion of the internal instruction which defines an operation; they are therefore called operation codes. The symbols E, S, and D represent locations in memory where data are to be stored.

Symbolic machine language corresponds closely to internal machine code. Other languages exist which allow the programmer to describe computational procedures in a code which corresponds more closely to the mathematical or natural expression of the procedure, and less closely to the internal instructions. These languages are commonly called *higher-level languages* (higher than symbolic machine language). The most widely used of these is FORTRAN, which permits coding in an algebra-like notation. The FORTRAN code that corresponds to the instructions described above takes the form of the single formula, or statement:

$$D = (E + S) / 2$$

This statement will be automatically translated into the internal machine code already described. The FORTRAN programmer need not concern himself with the assignment of memory locations to data items.

8. *Programs in Memory; Subprograms*

Now let us consider once more the sense of the word 'program.' A computer program specifies a procedure for performing a transformation or a set of transformations upon input data. During the execution of the program, the instructions which comprise it reside in the memory of the computer, along with data -- including input data, intermediate values computed by the program, and the final results which are to be the output.

We can think of memory as divided up into small cells, each of which contains an instruction or an item of data. Each of these cells, called *memory locations*, has associated with it a unique address. By referring to the address, we can get at the information, either to obtain a data item or to direct the control unit to execute an instruction stored at the specified location. We can also use the address to specify where a new item of information is to be stored. Memory can be visualized as shown in Figure 1.8.

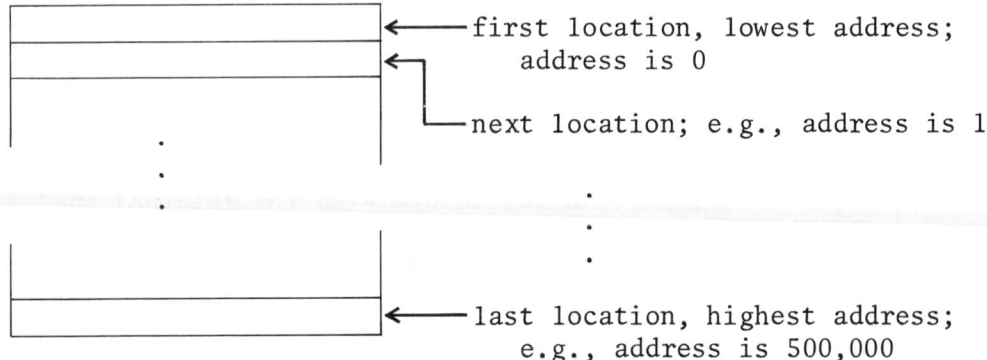

Figure 1.8

The way addresses are described depends on the particular machine. The address of the last location in memory will depend also on the memory size of the particular machine.

We can also think of memory as divided into blocks, each consisting of an arbitrary number of memory locations. One of these blocks may be occupied by a program. The block will consist of as many locations as the program requires. A program will require locations for its instruction sequence and for the relevant data items. When we speak of a complete program we normally imply that it is largely self-contained within a block of memory. That is, whatever data items are referred to by the instructions lie in the same memory block as the instructions themselves, and any transfers of control, or branches, within the program are to instructions which lie within the same block. Notice, however, that word 'largely' in the sentence before last.

In fact, when you have a computation to be performed by the computer this computation, or set of transformations upon data, is carried out by a group of *several* programs, which reside simultaneously in various blocks of memory. Each program performs a particular section of the job. You may write a program in one of the available programming languages; when your program is executed, a number of other programs will automatically be brought into memory to assist in the job. You may or may not be aware of the existence of these other programs, or of the need for them; in your program you may or may not have explicitly stipulated their use.

It is common to refer to these cooperating programs, including the program you have written, as *subprograms*. The exact distinction between a program and a subprogram is neither very clear nor very important. Each subprogram is largely self-contained in the sense described above. If they are to cooperate, however, there must be some communication or interaction between them. This communication can be accomplished according to certain programming conventions which will not be discussed here.

The state of the memory during the execution of a particular computation may be visualized as shown in Figure 1.9. One of the subprograms may be, for example, a program you have written; another may be concerned with the input of data from an external medium; another may be associated with bringing your program into memory in the first place; others may be available for the evaluation of such standard functions as square roots, sines, and cosines that may be required by your program.

In summary, then: In order to use a computer to carry out your computational needs, you may write a program in one of several programming languages. Alternatively, you may use a program written by someone else, e.g., a standard program made available by the computer manufacturer or by other users of the computer. You may also specify that other subprograms be brought into memory with yours to perform auxiliary functions. And finally, still others will be brought in without the necessity for any action on your part. The execution of this complex of subprograms will, it is hoped, result in the solution of the original problem.

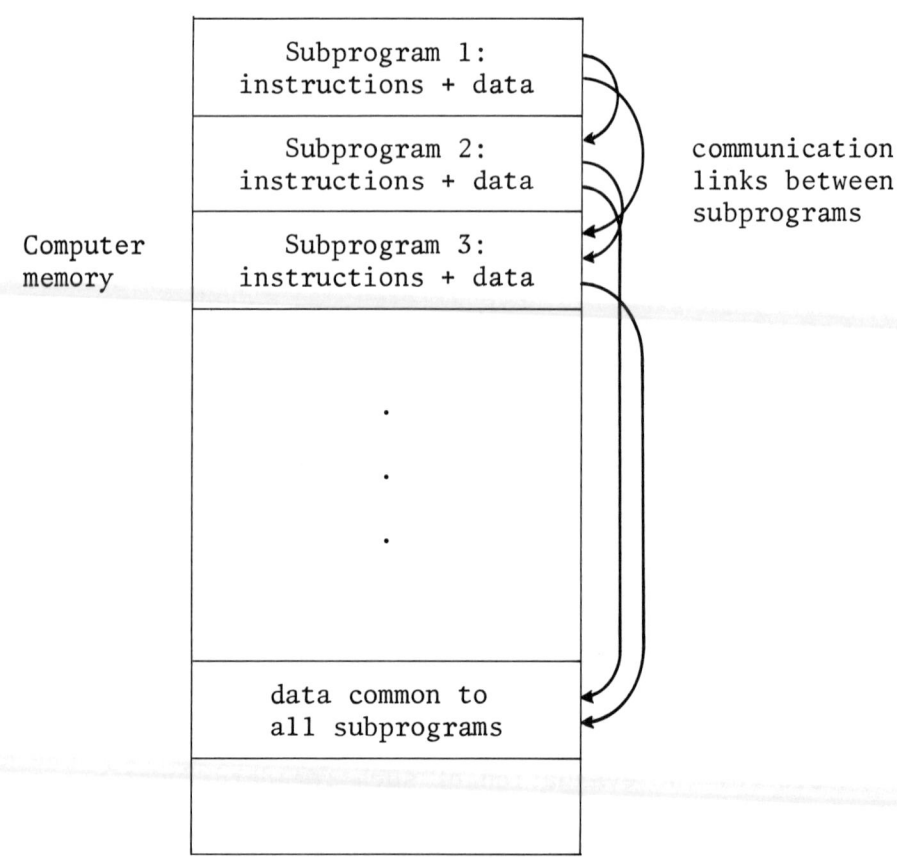

Figure 1.9

CHAPTER 2

STEPS IN COMPUTER PROBLEM-SOLVING

In order to demonstrate the steps that lie between the statement of a problem in ordinary language and its solution by computer, let us consider an example in some detail. We will follow this example through five phases in this chapter: problem definition, analysis, computational procedure, flow diagram, and coding. In later chapters we will pursue two final phases: running the program and interpreting the results. The problem requires some background information which may be stated in English, as may the problem itself.

Phase 1: Statement of the Problem (Definition)

Oceanographers frequently use acoustical devices for determining the depth of the ocean floor and of geologic strata underlying the floor. Following principles similar to those of radar detection, they direct a sharp sound-impulse toward the bottom of the ocean and measure the amount of time that elapses before an echo is returned from the bottom. Sometimes two ships are used for experiments of this type; one ship transmits the sonic impulse and the other ship receives the echo.

Figure 2.1 is a diagram of a situation where a number of simplifying assumptions have been made. Two ships, *Research Vessel Atalanta* and *R.V. Behemoth*, are positioned at A and B, respectively. The *Atalanta* is transmitting and the *Behemoth* is receiving (listening), both using devices called transducers that are attached to the hull of each ship. The ships are at a known distance from each other, represented by c, which is measured in feet.

The sound transmitted by the *Atalanta* actually travels in all directions, but the strongest echo will be received from sound striking the bottom at the angle α and being reflected at an equal angle up to the *Behemoth*. The distance traveled by this sound is represented by the lines marked a and b, which are not known in advance. The depth of the ocean floor is represented by d, which is the quantity we want to determine.

If the crew of the *Behemoth* know when the sound-impulse was emitted from the *Atalanta*, they can record the amount of time it took for the echo to reach them. This is the time for sound to travel the distance $(a + b)$. If we know the velocity of sound in sea water, we can use this knowledge to figure out the distance $(a + b)$. Can we also compute the distance d?

This is the problem stated in English, with the aid of a diagram. It is a computational problem, and it will be a repetitive one. The bottom echo must be measured many thousands of times, at many different points in the ocean. In order to make a topographic map of the ocean floor, computations of this type really are performed, although the real situation is considerably more complex.

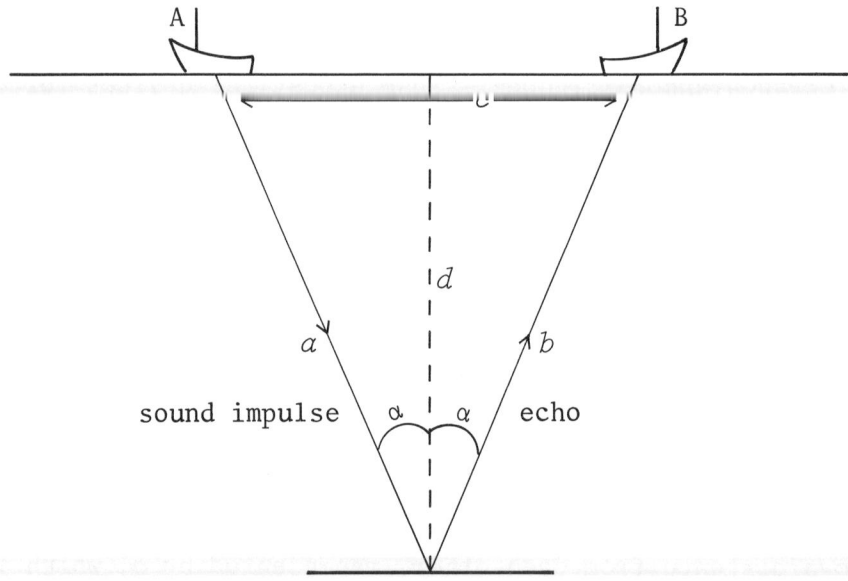

Figure 2.1

So far, however, we cannot go ahead and compute the depth d. We cannot yet write out instructions for a desk calculator or for a computer, describing the steps necessary for computing d. First we must analyze the problem, in this case using geometry, in order to arrive at a method of solution.

Phase 2: Analysis of the Problem

A reasonable first step in problem analysis is to see what we know to start with: what is given, or what facts can be regarded as input to the problem? The general statement of the problem reveals two such facts, or data: for a particular instance, we expect to have a value for c, the distance between the ships, in feet; and we will have a measure of the elapsed time between the transmission of the sound and the reception of the echo. We will call this time t, and assume that it's given in seconds.

It was also pointed out above that we can assume that we know how fast sound travels in sea water. Actually the velocity of sound varies with many factors, such as the temperature of the water, but for this example we will simply use an approximate figure, 4920 feet per second. Now if the sound travels the distance $(a + b)$ in t seconds, we can use the formula *distance equals velocity multiplied by time* to compute the distance $(a + b)$.

$$a + b = 4920 \times t \qquad (1)$$

Now let's look at the geometry of the problem. Figure 2.2 is a simplification of Figure 2.1.

In case you don't remember your geometry, the facts are these: The two triangles ACD and BCD are congruent right triangles; from this it follows that the lines AC and CB are equal, and a and b are equal.

The line AC + CB is what we have called c in Figure 2.1. Since AC = CB, the distance AC must equal $c/2$. We know the value of c, so now we know the length of AC.

We know we can compute $(a + b)$; it's $4920 \times t$, and t was given. Since $a = b$, then a is equal to $(a + b)/2$.

Let's review what we know. The right triangle ACD has hypotenuse equal to a, one leg equal to $c/2$, and the other leg equal to d, the object of our inquiry. Thanks to Pythagoras, we know that the square of the hypotenuse is equal to the sum of the squares of the other two sides. Or

$$a^2 = d^2 + (c/2)^2 \qquad (2)$$

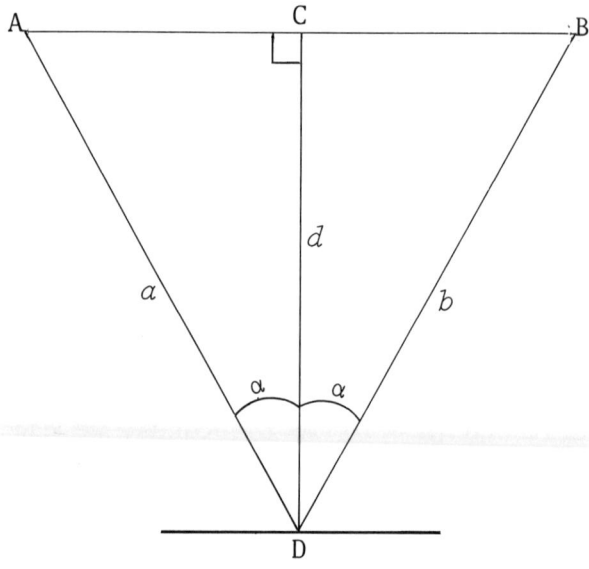

Figure 2.2

Discreet juggling of this equation (we turn now from geometry to algebra) yields the following:

$$d^2 = a^2 - (c/2)^2 \qquad (3)$$

$$d = \sqrt{a^2 - (c/2)^2} \qquad (4)$$

which means we can find d if we know a and c. But c was given, in feet. And since we have already determined that

$$a + b = 4920 \times t \qquad (1)$$

where t is given, in seconds, and also that

$$a = (a + b)/2 \qquad (5)$$

we can substitute in equation (5) and write

$$a = (4920 \times t)/2 \tag{6}$$

Applying (6) to (4), we now write

$$d = \sqrt{[(4920 \times t)/2]^2 - (c/2)^2} \tag{7}$$

which expresses d in terms of the input data, c and t. That's what we wanted all along. If we know c and t, we can find d.

Equation (7) provides a method of solution. Having once gone through the analysis of the problem, i.e., all the geometric and algebraic manipulations required to produce equation (7), we don't, clearly, need to go through them again every time we compute a value of d. We don't have to think any more, in fact. We simply plug into the equation the appropriate values of the known variables.

We know that d can be computed, and we have an equation describing its solution.

Phase 3: Computational Procedure

The transition from a theoretical analysis of the problem to a practical method of computing results will be trivial for some problems and of significant complexity for others. The analysis phase may result in mathematical expressions which, although unambiguous, do not immediately indicate a solution in terms of purely arithmetic operations. Since the computer's basic mathematical capability is arithmetic, it is sometimes necessary to devise ways of reducing more complicated formulas to arithmetic, or of approximating non-numerical expressions by numerical ones.

Fortunately much work has already been done in the development of computer techniques for various types of problems. Many *general-purpose programs* have been written and are available to everyone. By a general-purpose program we mean a program that can be used to solve a variety of problems of a particular type. For example, a programmer, in the course of solving a problem, might develop a method of evaluating the sine function for a certain angle, A; if his program will only compute the sine of A, it is a special-purpose program. If he were more farsighted, he would write a program which would compute the sine of any angle, accepting the value of A as input data; this would be a general-purpose program. It might also be practical for him to write a program to compute several of the trigonometric functions, so that the user of the program could specify as input both the value of the angle and the name of the particular function required.

Outlining a computational procedure for our oceanographic problem doesn't present any difficulties. The easiest way to grasp what is required is to imagine that you are going to present the data to an assistant who operates a desk calculator. Along with the data you must provide the operator with a step-by-step procedure for solving the equation, i.e., a 'desk calculator program.'

$$d = \sqrt{[(4920 \times t)/2]^2 - (c/2)^2}$$

1. Read from a table the values of the input: t and c.

2. Divide c by 2.

3. Multiply the result of step 2 by itself; save this value, $(c/2)^2$.

4. Multiply t by 4920.

5. Divide the result by 2.

6. Multiply the result of step 5 by itself.

7. Subtract $(c/2)^2$ from the result of step 6.

8. Take the square root of the result of step 7.

9. Write the result of step 8 as the value of d; this is the output, or final result, of the computation.

10. Repeat from step 1 as long as there are more input data.

Of particular interest is step 8. In order to calculate a square root on a desk calculator, one makes use of a standard procedure (which is often described in the calculator manual). An experienced calculator operator will usually be familiar with this procedure, which consists of a set of repeated, ordered arithmetic operations. The procedure is essentially a calculator program or subprogram which is to be executed at a particular point during the execution of the main program. Since it is a standard procedure familiar to the operator, we need only refer to it by *name*, 'square root,' in order to instruct the operator to make use of this particular subprogram.

In writing a computer program we can also use subprograms within other programs. We can make use of standard prewritten programs by referring to them by name. For example, in a FORTRAN program we can write

$$A = SQRT (R)$$

This statement specifies that A is to be set equal to the square root of R; for computing the square root, a standard subprogram named SQRT is to be brought into memory. The program SQRT will be one of the various subprograms which will aid the main FORTRAN program in solving a problem (compare Chapter 1, Section 8).

If we were going to write our program in symbolic machine language, the instructions would probably correspond roughly to the steps of the desk calculator program. This problem, however, readily lends itself to the use of a higher-level language like FORTRAN, and it is FORTRAN that we will use in the coding phase. Before preparing the coded program itself, we must complete one more step, the development of a flow diagram.

Phase 4: Flow Diagram

Phase 4 is closely linked to Phase 3, and the two are very often performed at the same time. The flow diagram is used in place of the numbered steps illustrated above. In the process of drawing a flow chart we discover whether any computational difficulties exist, so that Phase 3 is often simply a mental process accompanying Phase 4.

You are already familiar with flow diagrams, so study Figure 2.3 and observe how it describes the computational procedure. It differs from the desk calculator program in several respects: steps 2 through 8 have been condensed back into a single equation, and a few other steps have been added.

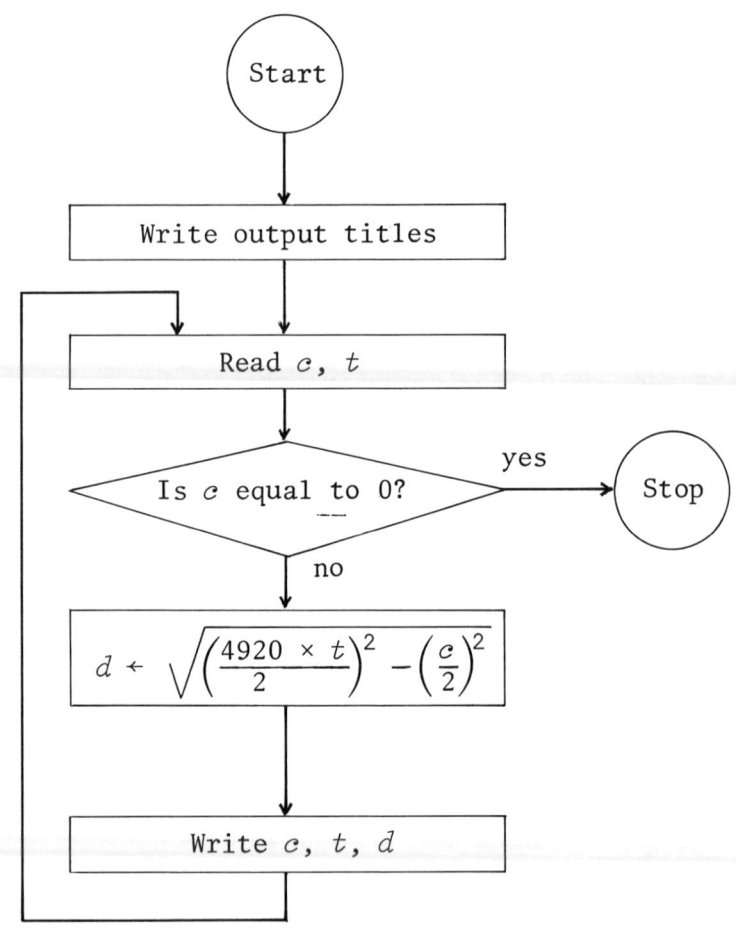

Figure 2.3

We will adhere to a few simple conventions for flow charts. A flow chart is made up of boxes, each containing the description of a procedure. A computation is enclosed in a rectangle;

an input or output step is also enclosed in a rectangle, with the words 'Read' or 'Write' used to identify it. A decision is enclosed in a diamond or lozenge shape. The boxes are connected by arrows that indicate the flow of control. Each box has at least one arrow leading into it. Decision boxes have two arrows leading out, while other boxes have one and only one arrow leading out.

There are also circles which represent terminals. The beginning of a program is indicated by a "Start" terminal and the end by a "Stop."

Returning to Figure 2.3, we see that the first box contains the words "Write output titles." The output of a program is normally printed on paper by a special printer associated with the computer. It is possible in a program to specify regular alphabetic text to be printed in addition to your computed results. This is very useful for identifying the results, as a list of numbers without adequate identification may be of no value at all.

We will write a title line describing the nature of the problem, and then a line of column headers to identify the numbers that will appear in the columns below:

```
    ATALANTA - BEHEMOTH DEPTH CALCULATIONS
RANGE (FEET)        ECHO (SECONDS)        DEPTH (FEET)
```

We use the titles RANGE and ECHO because they're more suggestive than 'c' and 't,' and we are careful to record the unit of measurement. Since the titles are to be written at the top of the page and will appear only once, we write them out first. Notice that the flow diagram shows clearly that control never returns to the box "Write output titles," so this step will be executed only once.

The next box, "Read c, t," has two arrows entering it; in other words, it can be reached by two different paths. It is entered by the straight line path from the beginning of the program, and by the loop from the bottom of the diagram. Every time this step is executed, two numbers will be read in as the values of c and t. In Chapter 4 we will see how the input values are supplied to the computer. If, for example, they are on punched cards, one of these cards will be read every time the statement "Read c, t" is executed.

In the decision box we ask whether the value of c on the card just read is equal to zero. This gives us an easy way to indicate where to terminate the program. We want to stop when there are no more data. If each set of values of c and t goes on one card, we can put at the end of the set of data cards an extra card which gives zero as the value of c. When this card is read, the program will be terminated.

If c is not zero, we proceed to compute d. Then we write out the result, along with the input values, so as to be able to correlate the results with the data. Every time the step "Write c, t, d" is executed, a line of printing will result, consisting of the numeric values of these variables. These numbers, then, will appear in the form of a table.

After this step we go back to read another card.

Phase 5: Coding the Program

The following program is coded in FORTRAN, and corresponds to the flow diagram of Figure 2.3. Each line is called a FORTRAN *statement*, and each has a statement number on the left.

```
1       PRINT 7
2       READ 8, C, T
3       IF (C .EQ. 0) STOP
4       D = SQRT ((4920 *T/2)**2 - (C/2)**2)
5       PRINT 9, C, T, D
6       GO TO 2
7       FORMAT ('1      ATALANTA - BEHEMOTH DEPTH CALCULATIONS'//
       .' RANGE (FEET)      ECHO (SECONDS)       DEPTH (FEET)'//)
8       FORMAT(F6.0,F6.2)
9       FORMAT(T4,F6.0,T26,F4.2,T42,F6.0)
10      END
```

Statement 1 is the first statement that will be executed. (Note that there is no statement corresponding to the 'start' of the flow diagram.) Statement 1 causes writing of the titles. The word PRINT means just what it says. The number 7 refers to statement number 7, which describes the format of what is to be printed. If you look at statement 7, you will see that the titles we want are there, along with some extra characters which are required. Statement 7 takes up two lines; the period appearing at the beginning of the second line indicates that this line is a continuation.

Statement 2 is an instruction to read input. The 8 refers to statement 8, which describes the format of the numbers on the card; we will not go any further into the nature of FORMAT statements in this text. The letters C, T indicate that the numbers read from the card are to be stored as the values of two variables named C and T respectively.

Now the names of these variables are arbitrary; we could just as well have called them RANGE and ECHO if we chose. The important thing about the name is that it is what we use when we want to get hold of a number. Once we have written the READ statement as it is above, we have defined a variable C, as well as directing that the first piece of data on the card is to be the current value of C. From now on in this program, whenever we refer to C we will get the number which was most recently assigned to that variable. This use of names is termed *symbolic reference*. The symbolic name 'C' actually refers in this program to a location in memory. The READ statement causes a number to be stored at that location, and any subsequent references to C will refer to that same location, either getting the number stored there, or putting a new number in its place.

Statement 3 refers to C and therefore will examine the number just read in from the data card. This statement says: If the value of C is equal to (.EQ.) zero, stop executing the program; otherwise, continue to the next statement (4).

Statement 4 defines a variable D and gives it a value equal to the value of the expression on the right of the equals sign. This is an arithmetic expression. Here's where all the computing gets done. First of all, there's some unfamiliar notation: a single asterisk means 'multiply'; a double asterisk means 'raise to a power.' To make the latter a little clearer, X**3 is the FORTRAN way of writing X^3. If there are parentheses around what precedes the double asterisk, then any operations inside the parentheses will be performed before raising the result to the desired power. Thus

$$(4920*T/2)**2$$

says, in effect: multiply T by 4920; divide by two; square the result.

Parentheses are used to make sure that the computations are done in the right order, just as in algebra. In statement 4 there are 'nested' parentheses. The first open parenthesis after SQRT matches the last close parenthesis at the very end of the statement. After everything inside these parentheses is done, we want to take the square root of the result. When our program is about to be executed, a subprogram called SQRT will automatically be brought into memory with it. During execution, when control reaches statement 4, the expression between the first and last parentheses will be evaluated. The resulting value will be transmitted to the subprogram SQRT, and control will pass to SQRT. The subprogram will compute the square root of the transmitted value and will in turn transmit the result back to our program; it will also pass control back to our program. The execution of statement 4 will then be completed by storing this result at the location represented by D.

Note that FORTRAN uses the equals sign instead of the left arrow to indicate assignment of a value to a variable.

Statement 5 causes printing of the current values of the three variables. The current values of C and T will be those read by the last execution of statement 2; the current value of D will be that computed by the last execution of statement 4.

Statement 6 executes unconditional transfer of control to statement 2. A new card will then be read, and the process repeated.

Statements 7 through 9 have already been touched on. Statement 10, the END statement, merely indicates that there are no more statements in the program. Notice that it does not mark the point where execution of the program will be terminated; this point is indicated by the STOP in statement 3.

This completes the preparation of a computer program for solving the problem described at the beginning of the chapter. We will return to this program later to discuss the mechanics of submitting it to the computer for execution.

EXERCISES

2.1 Let's look again at the flow diagram you developed in Exercise 1.8 of Chapter 1 (repeated on page 45). This diagram is complete, but it could be improved upon by several additions. First, we should consider the generality of the program; second, the possibility of elegant printed output.

As it stands, the program will read one card, containing a single value for R and a single value for N; the sum of the first N terms will be computed and printed out; then the program will be terminated. Now if this program is of any value at all, it will be used many times, for many R's and N's. The reasoning behind this runs as follows. Since every programmer makes programming and coding mistakes, the results of a program are usually checked by hand, if possible. If a program computes answers for only one set of data, and the answers are hand-checked for those data, then nothing has been gained by using the computer. There is a gain only after we know that the answers are right for one set and can fairly safely assume that they will be right for many other sets.

The logical thing to do, then, is to modify the program so that after it prints out a value of S it will go back and read another data card. Since the phrase 'go back' immediately introduces another loop into the program, we must also introduce another decision box so that we have a means of terminating the loop. Our input data will be a set of punched cards, each with a pair of values, R and N. It might again be convenient to put at the end of this set of cards a card giving zero as the value of R. Then the program can terminate whenever it finds the condition R = 0.

Notice that there will be nothing in the program that defines or restricts the number of data cards we can use, i.e., the number of times this new loop will be executed. This type of generality is often very useful. Notice also, however, that we take advantage of a special characteristic of the problem: namely, that the program is of no interest for R = 0.

Since we are going to print out more than one value of S, it seems sensible to print out the values of R and N associated with each S. Furthermore, we will want to identify each number. We can arrange to have the output in tabular form, with a single alphabetic line at the top to identify each column.

Now, redraw the flow diagram, making two modifications:

(a) Introduce a loop so that data cards will be read and the computation repeated until R = 0.
(b) Modify the output so that R, N, and S will be printed, and insert a title line at the top.

Check your answer before going on.

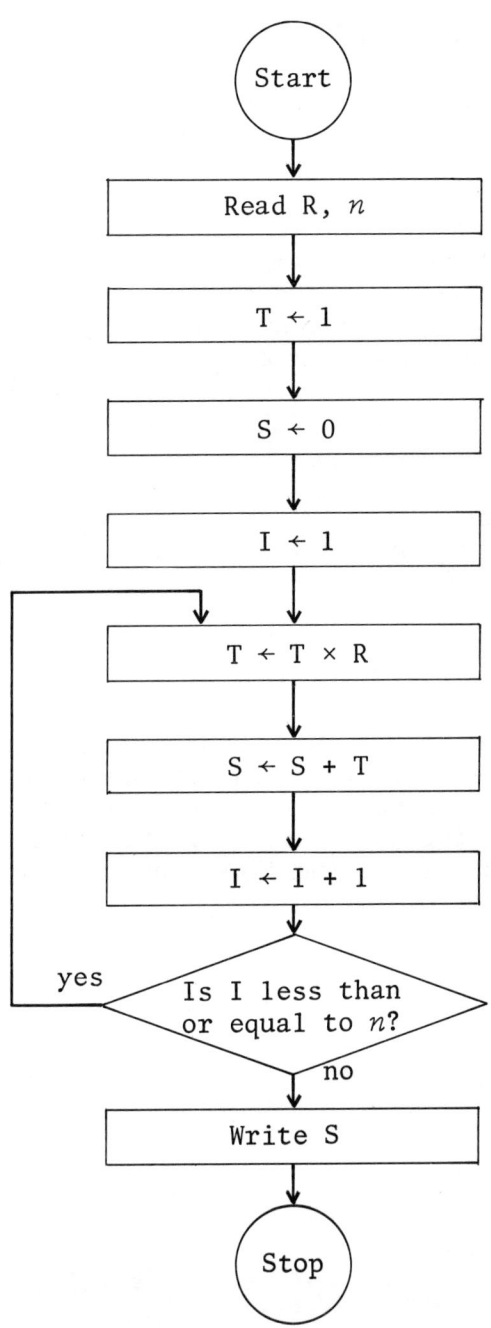

2.2   On the basis of the flow diagram of Exercise 2.1, assemble a FORTRAN program from the list of FORTRAN statements on the next page. These statements all conform to the rules for legal or syntactically correct statements, but some of them will work for this program and some will not.

Notice that only some of the statements are numbered. We used numbers in the earlier example as a convenient way of referring to the statements in the text. Numbers may always be used, but they are only *required* when the program itself needs to refer to a statement, as for example in expressing a transfer of control. If we write GO TO 17 there must be a statement with the number 17, and we expect control to be transferred to that statement.

Select from the list only those statements that will work, using the flow diagram as a guide. Write them out in correct order, taking note of the fact that every character, including commas and periods, is essential. Note also that the order in which statements are written is *all-important*, as it governs the flow of control of the program.

(Note: just as the symbol .EQ. stands for 'is equal to,' the symbol .LE. stands for 'is less than or equal to.' Note also that the statement numbered 13 takes up two lines; the period at the beginning of the second line identifies it as a continuation of the first. These two lines must not be separated.)

	T=1
	T=T+1
7	T=T*R
7	T=T*S
	S=T
	S=0
	S=S+T
	S=1
3	I=1
	I=I+1
	I=I
	I=1
	IF (I .EQ. N) GO TO 7
2	IF (R .EQ. 0) GO TO 7
	IF (R .EQ. 0) STOP
	IF (I .LE. N) GO TO 7
7	END
	END
	GO TO 2
	GO TO 3
13	FORMAT ('1 GEOMETRIC SERIES'//
	.' BASE NO. TERMS SUM'//)
14	FORMAT (F5.2,I5)
15	FORMAT (F7.2,I9,6X,F11.8)
	PRINT 13
	PRINT 13,R,N
7	PRINT 13
	PRINT 15,R,N,SUM
	PRINT 15,R,N,S
2	READ 14,R,N,S
2	READ 14,R,N

Check your answer before going on.

CHAPTER 3

INFORMATION STORAGE AND PROCESSING

Now that we have an idea of what is involved in programming for a computer, let us take a closer look at some of the computer components and operations that have already been mentioned briefly. We will discuss the IBM 360 in particular, but what we are going to describe applies, at least qualitatively, to most other modern digital computers.

1. *Memory Structure: Terminology*

The *memory* is the computer component that retains information, either programs or data. The memory can hold many items of information, with each item stored at an identifiable location. The entire memory unit is divided into cells, called memory *registers*. Associated with each memory register is a unique number, called its *address*; the address identifies the location of a register.

When an item of information is stored in the memory, it occupies one or more registers. When we want to retrieve an item of information from the memory, the most direct and explicit way to do so is to specify the address of the register or registers that contain it: "Get me the information stored in 4 registers beginning with register 599." In actual practice, we don't usually use addresses, because that's an inconvenient way to refer to information; we would rather say "Get me the value of X." As we shall see, however, the phrase "the value of X" can represent -- that is, can be translated into -- "the information stored beginning at register 599."

Each memory register holds a piece of information. Whatever information is stored in a register at any time is called the *contents* of that register. Different types of computers have memories with different kinds of organization, and the size of a memory register differs from one to another. So does the terminology used to describe registers and their contents. Generally, however, we can be safe in calling a memory register the smallest addressable unit of memory, that is, the smallest piece of memory that has a unique address.

In 360 terminology, the memory register is often called a memory *location*, and its *contents* are called a *byte*. We'll come back to bytes later on. Another important term is *word*. In the 360, four adjacent bytes make up a word. It turns out that for many kinds of information, four bytes is a natural and useful amount of information to consider as a unit, even though it occupies four distinct memory registers.

Throughout this text, we will frequently use the terms *word*, *memory register*, and *location*. We will refer to *bytes* only when it is necessary to discuss the component parts of words in memory.

A word in memory may be either an instruction or an item of data. Here we are using *data* in a rather more general sense than is normally implied. In computer terminology, we describe as data all information words in the memory that are not instructions. Thus we include numbers and alphabetic information, whether they are input data or values computed by the program; we speak of 'input data,' 'intermediate data,' and 'output data.'

2. *The Central Processing Unit*

In addition to the memory, there are a number of special registers in the computer which comprise what is known as the *central processing unit* or CPU. The CPU embraces the arithmetic unit and the control unit, and most arithmetic and control functions are executed in the special CPU registers.

The interaction between the CPU and the memory rests on two basic operations, *fetch* and *store*. The contents of a memory register may be fetched by the CPU to a special register, and the contents of a special register may be stored into a memory register. Most other operations, including both the interpretation of instruction words and the arithmetic manipulation of data words, take place in the CPU.

An important aspect of the fetch and store operations is that when a word is fetched from memory it is copied into the

CPU register while the word remains unchanged in memory. That is, fetching is *non-destructive* with respect to memory. When a word is stored into a memory register, however, the original contents of the memory register is over-written. Thus the store operation is *destructive* with respect to memory.

This is a very important point to remember. It illuminates, for example, the FORTRAN statement

$$I = I + 1$$

which was encountered earlier. Here I represents a memory register that contains the value of a variable named I. If the current value of I is 2, then this memory register contains a word representing the number 2. When the FORTRAN statement is executed, this word will be brought into a CPU register. At this point I still contains 2, since fetching is non-destructive. Next, another word, representing the number 1, will be added to 2 in the CPU, producing the sum, 3. This new word will now be stored into the location represented by I, and the old contents of I will be destroyed.

Notice here the facility, in FORTRAN as in other programming languages, for *symbolic reference*. When we refer in a FORTRAN statement to I, we use I to stand for the address of a memory register. Similarly we use the numeral 1 to stand for the address of a memory register that contains the number 1. This is a feature of the programming language, and not of the computer itself. We will see later how symbolic references become translated into machine language.

EXERCISE

3.1 Suppose that during the execution of a FORTRAN program the following sequence of statements is encountered:

```
37     ALPHA = 2
38     BETA = 5
39     ALPHA = ALPHA + BETA
```

These three statements contain altogether four symbolic references to memory registers containing information, to wit:

```
ALPHA
2
BETA
5
```

Suppose that these symbols refer to actual memory registers as follows:

```
ALPHA:  register 592
2    :  register 608
BETA :  register 612
5    :  register 642
```

The execution of statements 37 through 39 will cause changes in the contents of certain of these registers, as well as in one or more of the special CPU registers. On the next page is a table showing the initial state of these registers. Fill in the rest of the table, showing the state of the registers after the completion of each statement.

Register	Before Statement 37	After Statement 37	After 38	After 39
(CPU)	Unknown			
592	not yet defined			
608	2			
612	not yet defined			
642	5			

Check your answer before going on.

3. *Differentiation of Instruction and Data*

Now consider the FORTRAN statement:

GO TO 1

where 1 is the number, or statement label, of another FORTRAN statement. The statement with label 1 corresponds to a sequence of computer instructions. The first instruction of this sequence has an address, say 1065. The statement label 1 corresponds to this memory address, so that "GO TO 1" may correspond to "transfer control to location 1065."

The numeral 1 may thus mean two entirely different things in the same program, in that it may refer to either a data word or an instruction word. The distinction, clearly, is in the context. It is easy to tell that a "GO TO" statement requires the address of an instruction, while an arithmetic statement like "I = I + 1" requires the address of a data word.

In the actual memory of the computer there is no built-in distinction between instruction words and data words. They are distinguished only by what the CPU does with them.

The control section of the CPU includes a special register, called an instruction counter, that keeps track of the flow of control. At any moment, the instruction counter contains the address of an instruction; this is the instruction next to be executed. Normally instructions are executed in the order that they appear in memory. An instruction is fetched from the memory location specified by the address in the instruction counter. While the instruction is being interpreted and executed, the address in the instruction counter is stepped forward to the address of the next instruction in sequence. But if the current instruction is a transfer of control to some other sequence of instructions, the starting address of the new sequence will be inserted in the instruction counter.

For example, suppose that a FORTRAN statement has the (symbolic) statement label 16; and suppose that the sequence of instructions that correspond to this statement is stored in memory, beginning at location 4776. Then upon execution of the

FORTRAN statement "GO TO 16," the instruction counter would contain the address 4776.

Now, one way that a word can be fetched from memory to the CPU is if its address turns up in the instruction counter, as described above. On the other hand, the instruction being executed in the CPU may specify the address of another word. An *add* instruction, for example, specifies the address of a number that is to be added (to some other number). If the machine instruction is "Add 1197," the *operand* of the instruction is the word stored at location 1197. This word will be fetched from memory and treated as a data word.

Thus a word will be treated as an instruction if its address is specified in the instruction counter. On the other hand, if its address appears in the operand part of an instruction that is being executed, it is treated as a data word.

This implies that a word coded as an instruction might be treated as a data word, and operated on in some way. This very often happens, as it allows programs to be written that modify themselves by operating on their own instructions. Conversely, a word coded as a data word might be treated as an instruction and executed. This often happens too, and is usually a mistake; it happens when a transfer of control is incorrectly coded and control is erroneously transferred into an area of storage that contains data.

In spite of this danger, the intrinsic indistinguishability of memory words is one of the most powerful features of the computer. The difficulties presented are minor and are almost entirely eliminated by the use of symbolic programming language.

4. *Core Storage and Data*

The memory of most modern computers is made up of *magnetic cores*. A 360 memory address, for example, refers to a memory register, which is a group of eight of these cores. A core is a tiny ring of ferromagnetic material which can be magnetized in either a clockwise or a counter-clockwise direction. The two possible states of a core may be arbitrarily assigned to

represent two values; for example, plus and minus, or true and
false. Normally they are assigned the values one and zero. In
particular applications, a zero often represents plus, or false,
while a one represents minus, or true.

Since each core can be set to either of two values, then an
8-core register can represent any of the possible combinations
of 8 two-valued, or *binary*, digits. A binary digit, abbreviated
as *bit*, has either of the two values zero and one. If we had a
register consisting of two cores, the possible configurations
it could contain are:

$$00$$
$$01$$
$$10$$
$$11$$

Thus a total of four different items of data can be represented
by two bits. A three-core register could hold eight different
data items:

$$000$$
$$001$$
$$010$$
$$011$$
$$100$$
$$101$$
$$110$$
$$111$$

In general, n bits can collectively represent 2^n different
values; an 8-bit byte, such as we encounter in the 360, has 2^8,
or 256, possible values.

A 360 byte, then, is a particular configuration of 8 bits.
As we mentioned earlier, four of these bytes are often grouped
together to make a 360 word, of 32 bits in length. This 32-bit
word has 2^{32} possible values; 2^{32} is 4,294,967,296. A 360 word
can be visualized as in Figure 3.1. The 32 bit-positions of
the word are numbered from zero to 31. (In computer terminology
we very often begin numbering things from zero.)

bit position	0	1	2	3	4	5	...	29	30	31
	1	0	1	1	1	0	...	0	0	1

Figure 3.1

Using a binary code, with two-state storage devices such as the magnetic core, allows for a versatile and efficient computer. Virtually any kind of information can be broken down into a binary representation. The interpretation of a byte, or of a word, depends almost entirely on how we choose to make use of the information.

As a first example, consider the problem of representing whole decimal numbers, or integers, in memory. A 360 word allows for 2^{32} different configurations. This implies that a word could be used to represent any number from 1 to 4,294,967,296. If we want to have a way of representing zero, we can reserve one configuration for it -- a natural choice would be the word that consists of 32 zeros. We can thus represent zero and any positive decimal integer from 1 to 4,294,967,295 (which is 2^{32} - 1).

So far we have been considering only *how many* numbers we can represent, and not how they are to be represented (except for the zero). In fact, we have suggested that we can represent integers from 1 to 4,294,967,295, but even that is arbitrary. The point is that having reserved the all-zero word for zero, we have 2^{32} - 1 different *configurations* left, which we can use however we want. We could assign them, for example, to all the *even* integers from 2 to 8,589,934,590. It is certainly more natural, however, and potentially more useful, to give the assignment described first.

Suppose, however, that we want to be able to express both positive and negative integers. We need a way to represent the sign of the number. One way of doing this is to set aside one bit -- say, the bit in position zero -- for the sign. If the zero position bit is zero, we will regard the number as positive; if it is one, the number will be negative. (See Figure 3.2.) This means we have only 31 bits left for the number.

bit position	S	1	2	3	4	...	29	30	31	
	0	0	1	0	0	...	1	1	1	positive integer
	1	0	1	0	0	...	1	1	1	negative integer

Figure 3.2

Following the same formula we used before (n bits allows 2^n different patterns), we find that we can represent 2^{31}, or 2,147,483,648, different numbers, each with a sign that may be plus or minus. Again, the natural way to assign the available bit patterns will be to reserve the all-zero pattern for zero, and assign the rest to the integers from -2,147,483,647 to +2,147,483,647.

EXERCISES

3.2 Imagine a computer with a word-length of four bits -- that is, a computer with memory registers made up of four cores. Write out all the possible states -- or configurations of bits -- of such a register.

3.3 It was stated earlier that n bits can collectively have 2^n different states. Verify this formula, by Exercise 3.2, for the case $n = 4$.

3.4 Herman Hollerith, inventor of the punched card (sometimes, rather unfairly, known as the IBM card), is said to have been inspired by watching a train conductor using a punch to record passenger fares. A card with clearly defined positions which may be either punched or not punched is analogous to a computer memory register and is fundamentally a device for binary representation of information.

Suppose that we have such a card, and that four positions are set aside for encoding a particular piece of information -- say, for recording the town to which a passenger is traveling. This four-position field, as it's called, is analogous to our hypothetical four-core register.

A straightforward way to use this field to record passenger destinations would be to assign a town to each position. The code might be:

```
punch in position 1 : Bala-Cynwyd
punch in position 2 : Manayunk (as illustrated)
punch in position 3 : Conshohocken
punch in position 4 : Norristown
```

which would suffice for a four-stop train.

- (a) Assume that a single destination is represented by a unique arrangement of punches in the four-position field illustrated above. By putting any amount of strain on the conductor, what is the maximum number of towns that could be represented in this field?

- (b) What is the fundamental difference between the illustrated method for a four-stop train and a method that would allow more towns to be represented?

- (c) Can you devise a coding scheme that would put relatively little strain on the conductor and allow the representation of exactly six towns?

3.5   The four-bit word can be used to represent integers, following the scheme described in the text: zero is represented by the all-zero word; the left-most bit is reserved for the sign. What range of integers could we represent, using the 'natural' assignment described earlier?

Check your answers before going on.

Before going on to describe how we make the correspondence between particular bit-patterns and particular integers, there are two points which need to be cleared up. First, let's consider the simpler 4-bit case of Exercise 3.5. There are sixteen available bit patterns, to wit:

Positive		*Negative*	
0000	0100	1000	1100
0001	0101	1001	1101
0010	0110	1010	1110
0011	0111	1011	1111

The range of integers that our scheme provides is -7 to +7. But that is only fifteen different numbers: -7, -6, -5, -4, -3, -2, -1, 0, 1, 2, 3, 4, 5, 6, 7. How is it that we've assigned only fifteen out of the sixteen available patterns?

The answer is that if we follow the scheme as developed above, we've allowed two patterns for each number pair: +7 and -7, +6 and -6, and so forth, including +0 and -0. This last doesn't make sense, however, since zero has no sign. But we can preserve the relative simplicity of the scheme by simply treating both patterns as equivalent to zero. In some computers (the IBM 7094, for example) this is what is done.

The other point that has to be established at this stage is that there are other ways of representing signed integers, and that the scheme described here is *not* normally used in the 360. The difference, however, is not such as to be of any concern here. Most people who use computers don't need to know exactly how information is represented. What is important is to understand the general principles of binary encoding of information; the foregoing example will serve as well as another, and has some advantage of simplicity.

We will be able to represent numbers, then, according to some binary code. Another binary code will be used to represent computer instructions. Inasmuch as the distinction between instruction words and data words depends on how they are used, there is no reason why a particular configuration of bits cannot represent both a number and a specific computer instruction. There is no ambiguity in practice, since usage determines the meaning; but if we look at an isolated computer word there is no way to determine whether it is instruction or data.

5. *Positional Number Systems*

As we pointed out earlier, we made no mention of how we would assign a particular bit-pattern to a particular number, except for the case of the representation of zero. We should be able to find something better than an arbitrary code relating bit-configurations and decimal numbers. It ought to be possible to do arithmetic with these words, and it should also be possible to interpret a binary word according to a logical rule rather than by arbitrary associations. What is used is the *binary number system*, a system of counting and arithmetic that is similar to the familiar decimal number system but involves only the digits 0 and 1.

The *decimal* or *Arabic number system*, which we normally use, is a method of representing numbers based on the *position* of digits relative to a special symbol, the decimal point. A digit can have one of ten possible values, from zero through 9. Any number greater than nine, as well as any number that is not an integer, is represented as a string of digits. The position of each digit relative to the decimal point indicates the *power of ten* by which that digit is to be multiplied. For example, the decimal number 214.6 is really:

$$200 + 10 + 4 + 6/10$$

that is,

$$(2 \times 10^2) + (1 \times 10^1) + (4 \times 10^0) + (6 \times 10^{-1}).$$

If this notation is unfamiliar, let us review for a moment the rules for writing exponents.

$10^2 = 10 \times 10$

$n^2 = n \times n$, no matter what value n has.

$n^p = n \times n \times \ldots \times n$, where n appears p times.

$10^1 = 10$

$n^1 = n$

$10^0 = 1$ This may not make any sense intuitively, so it can be regarded as an arbitrary convention.

$n^0 = 1$

$n^{-1} = 1/n$ Again, if this seems meaningless, regard it as a convention of mathematics.

$n^{-2} = 1/n^2$

$n^{-p} = 1/n^p$

Now, returning to our decimal number 214.6, we can break it down as follows:

$$200 = 2 \times 10^2$$
$$+ \quad 10 = 1 \times 10^1$$
$$+ \quad 4 = 4 \times 10^0$$
$$+ \quad .6 = 6 \times 10^{-1}$$

The first digit to the left of the decimal point is the multiplier of the zeroth power of 10, the second is the multiplier of the first power of 10, and so forth. In writing *integers*, we normally omit the decimal point. The integer 1965 may be written as a sum of powers of ten:

$$(1 \times 10^3) + (9 \times 10^2) + (6 \times 10^1) + (5 \times 10^0)$$

EXERCISES

3.6 Write the following expressions as ordinary decimal numbers:

(a) $(5 \times 10^2) + (9 \times 10^1) + (4 \times 10^0) + (7 \times 10^{-1})$

(b) $(3 \times 10^3) + (6 \times 10^1) + (8 \times 10^{-2})$

3.7 Write the following decimal numbers as sums of powers of ten.

(a) 7092
(b) 566.7
(c) .1104

Check your answers before going on.

The enormous advantage of a number system like ours is the ease with which arithmetic operations can be carried out. For example, in order to perform addition, all that we have to memorize is the sums of pairs of the digits 0 through 9; then the add-and-carry method can be applied. (The virtues of a positional system of notation are evident if you try to imagine a rule for addition using the Roman numeral system.) A variety of useful consequences fall out of the positional system: such as the fact that to multiply any number by 10 we simply shift the decimal point one place to the right; and to divide by 10, we shift the decimal point one place to the left.

It is important to realize, however, that the use of ten as the *base* of the number system is purely arbitrary. Ten and five have always been important in counting, as for example in the Roman system and in the old tally system, presumably because it was always convenient to use fingers for counting. But we could apply the principles of the Arabic number system to any base. The rules for constructing a general positional number system without specifying the base, which we will call b, are simple enough:

1. We require b numerals, from 0 through $b-1$ (e.g., if $b=10$, the numerals are 0 through 9).

2. The position of each digit with respect to the *point* determines the power of b by which the digit is to be the multiplied. Digit positions to the right of the point represent negative powers of b, while positions to the left represent nonnegative powers. The value of the number is the sum of the digits each multiplied by its respective power of b.

By way of illustration, suppose we choose eight as a base, and develop what would naturally be called an *octal* number system. With b equal to eight, we will need eight numerals to work with; it seems natural to choose the numerals 0, 1, 2, 3, 4, 5, 6 and 7. Building up a table of decimal numbers and their octal equivalents, we can start out with one-digit numbers as follows:

Decimal	Octal
0	0
1	1
2	2
3	3
4	4
5	5
6	6
7	7

Now in the decimal system, 8 means (8×10^0); but in the octal system, the next number after 7 is the base itself. The base, b, can be written as $(1 \times b^1) + (0 \times b^0)$, or 10. In fact, no matter what b is, the representation of b in a system with base b will always be 10, provided that the numerals 0 and 1 are employed in the usual way.

Let's distinguish octal numbers by writing them with a subscript, thus: 2047_8 is an octal number, while 2047_{10} is a number in the decimal system.

We have established that 8_{10} corresponds to 10_8. If the argument wasn't convincing, let's try it another way: Start with the number 10_8, and work out its decimal equivalent. To convert 10_8 to decimal, we expand it in decimal as:

$$(1 \times 8^1) + (0 \times 8^0)$$

which by decimal arithmetic reduces to 8_{10}.

As another example of octal-to-decimal conversion, let's take 2047_8 and expand it in decimal, thus:

$$
\begin{aligned}
2047 &= (2 \times 8^3) + (0 \times 8^2) + (4 \times 8^1) + (7 \times 8^0) \\
&= 2 \times 512 + 0 \times 64 + 4 \times 8 + 7 \times 1 \\
&= 1024 + 0 + 32 + 7 \\
&= 1063
\end{aligned}
$$

which demonstrates that according to the rules of the game,

octal 2047 is equivalent to decimal 1063.

Here is a continuation of the table of decimal-octal equivalents for two-digit numbers.

Decimal	Octal	Decimal	Octal
8	10	.	
9	11	.	
10	12	.	
11	13	61	75
12	14	62	76
13	15	63	77
14	16	64	100
15	17	65	101
16	20	66	102
17	21	67	103
18	22	68	104
.		.	
.		.	
.		.	

EXERCISES

3.8   Verify that the table on the preceding page is correct, by converting the octal numbers to decimal by the prescribed method.

3.9   How many numerals would be required for a number system with base sixteen?

3.10   In a number system with base sixteen (call it the *hexadecimal* system) consider the following numbers and find their decimal equivalents:

$$22_{16}, \ 10_{16}, \ 109_{16}.$$

Check your answers before going on.

3.11   Using the prescribed method for conversion from another base to decimal, and using the hexadecimal table of Exercise 3.9, find the decimal equivalents of the following hexadecimal numbers:

$$1F_{16}, \ C2_{16}, \ FF_{16}.$$

Check your answer before going on.

6. *The Binary Number System*

Now let us consider, for a moment, the design of a mechanical device for representing *decimal* numbers. One way to do this would be to have a series of wheels, each wheel having ten positions. Each wheel could then represent a digit with a value from 0 to 9. Five wheels in a row would allow us to represent a five-digit decimal number, as in Figure 3.3. The arrows indicate where the value of the digit is to be read from the wheel. The wheels are set in the figure to record the number 24790.

Figure 3.3

What can be said about an analogous device for a number system with a base other than ten? Since a number system with base b requires digits from 0 to $b-1$, a machine like the one of Figure 3.3 would require a wheel with b positions. In the design of a computing machine, this wheel (or an analogous device) would be the fundamental element, and its design would be of crucial importance. Under certain conditions we should perhaps design the wheel for maximum efficiency and economy, and let its optimum design determine the base of the number system that we will use.

In electrical or electronic machines it is very convenient to use devices that have only two *states*; for example, a switch may be on or off, a pulse may or may not pass through a circuit, a hole may or may not be punched in a particular area of a card. It is considerably more complicated to use a device that has ten states, like the decimal wheel of the illustration. The magnetic core described earlier in this chapter is a two-state device. It is analogous to a two-position wheel, or to a switch with two states -- on or off. If you imagine that *on* represents 1, and *off* represents 0, you will have a fair idea of what core memory is like: a lot of binary switches, set on or off, and grouped for convenience into blocks of various possible lengths.

Well, if the best information storage element has two states, we can use a number system that has two numerals: 0 and 1. Numbers can be represented in terms of powers of two. This binary number system ($b = 2$) is fundamental to most modern digital computers. Let's examine it briefly.

The number seven can be reduced to

$$4 + 2 + 1$$

and here each term is a power of two. We could rewrite it as

$$1 \times 2^2 = 4$$
$$1 \times 2^1 = 2$$
$$1 \times 2^0 = 1$$

Just as in the decimal system, we can dispense with writing '$\times 2^p$' in every case, if we let the *position* of the multiplier indicate the power of two which it is to multiply. Thus we write

$$111$$

where the 'point' (which we now call the binary point rather than the decimal point) is understood to be on the right.

Let's go back to re-examine the possible arrangements of four bits. Earlier, we presented a scheme whereby the leftmost bit would represent the sign, and the remaining three bits, an integer. The possible combinations of three bits are

```
000   (which we took to represent zero)
001
010       100       110
011       101       111
```

If we now regard these as instances of the binary number system, to what decimal representations do they correspond? The table below shows the correspondences.

Binary Representation	Corresponding Sum	Decimal Equivalent
000	$0 \times 2^2 + 0 \times 2^1 + 0 \times 2^0$	0
001	$0 \times 2^2 + 0 \times 2^1 + 1 \times 2^0$	1
010	$0 \times 2^2 + 1 \times 2^1 + 0 \times 2^0$	2
011	$0 \times 2^2 + 1 \times 2^1 + 1 \times 2^0$	3
100	$1 \times 2^2 + 0 \times 2^1 + 0 \times 2^0$	4
101	$1 \times 2^2 + 0 \times 2^1 + 1 \times 2^0$	5
110	$1 \times 2^2 + 1 \times 2^1 + 0 \times 2^0$	6
111	$1 \times 2^2 + 1 \times 2^1 + 1 \times 2^0$	7

EXERCISES

3.12   Using the binary integer coding scheme described earlier for a four-bit word, with the left-most bit representing the sign (0 for plus, 1 for minus), how would you represent the following decimal integers?

    (a)   3
    (b)   -5
    (c)   -2
    (d)   +6

3.13   By the same scheme, what are the decimal integer equivalents of the following binary numbers?

    (a)   1111
    (b)   0001
    (c)   0111
    (d)   1100

Check your answers before going on.

Returning to the use of a 32-bit (four-byte) word for integers, we can simply extend the scheme that we've developed for a 4-bit integer. The left-most bit (bit zero in the illustration) represents the sign. The remaining 31 bits represent the integer. The rightmost bit (bit 31) represents by a zero or one the multiplier of the zero power of two; bit 30 represents the multiplier of the first power of two, etc. Bit 1 represents the multiplier of the thirtieth power of two.

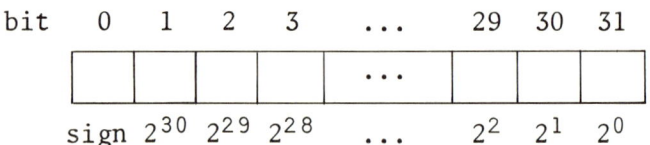

Figure 3.4

The largest number that can be represented in this word format is the number that has a one in all 31 places (just as the largest 4-digit decimal number is 9999, for example). This number is:

$(1 \times 2^{30}) + (1 \times 2^{29}) + (1 \times 2^{28}) + \ldots + (1 \times 2^1) + (1 \times 2^0)$

which is exactly one less than 2^{31}, i.e., 2,147,438,647 in decimal.

The binary number system supplies a convenient way of doing arithmetic by computer. It allows the use of simple two-way switches for the electronic storage and offers a relatively natural way of coding numbers in binary form. Furthermore, it implies an arithmetic, which is essentially similar to decimal arithmetic, and has the same - and additional - advantages. Addition, for example, can still be performed by the add-and-carry method. Note that:

$$1+0 = 1$$
$$0+1 = 1$$
$$0+0 = 0$$
$$1+1 = 10, \text{ or "zero and carry 1".}$$

Following the usual method of addition, we can see that

$$\begin{array}{r} 101 \\ +1 \\ \hline \text{yields } 110 \end{array}$$

and inspection of the table on page 70 will verify that this corresponds to 5 + 1 = 6.

Binary addition is simpler than decimal, particularly for a computing machine. We noted earlier that in order to add decimal numbers of any magnitude it is necessary to learn only the sums of pairs of the digits 0 through 9. In the binary system, one has to learn only the sums of pairs of the digits 0 and 1 which comes down to the four sums shown above.

Arithmetic instructions are built into the central processing unit of the computer that perform binary arithmetic in essentially the manner described. Subtraction, multiplication, and division are similarly easy. The simplicity of the binary system for both number representation and number manipulation is a major reason for the speed and economy of modern electronic computers.

7. *Hardware vis-a-vis Software*

In any discussion of the format of computer information storage and processing it is essential to observe a distinction between those capabilities, conventions, and restrictions that are built into the circuitry of the machine and those that are established by programming. Those features that are part of the circuitry and cannot be altered by programming are called *hardware characteristics* of the computer. Binary integer arithmetic is a hardware characteristic of the 360.

Let us introduce some more computer jargon in order to simplify the discussion. A research worker who has a particular problem to be solved using the computer will be referred to as a *user*. The program he writes, in FORTRAN for example, will be called a *user program* or *application program*.

Now a user is, of course, ultimately dependent upon the hardware for the execution of his program. But he does not operate with, so to speak, a naked computer. His program is executed in conjunction with and under the control of a complex system of other programs, which may be considered extensions of the basic hardware. These programs make up a *programming system*, or *operating system*, and are generally termed system programs.

For example, the FORTRAN user almost never needs to concern himself with the binary configuration of computer words. His program will consist of symbolic statements, such as:

$$A = X + 98$$

which include normal decimal numbers. The statements in his program are processed by one of the system programs, the FORTRAN *translator*, which converts the number 98 into proper binary form and also generates the internal machine code for performing the specified (binary) addition.

A user program undergoes a considerable amount of processing, both before and after the execution of instructions. This processing is automatic, under control of the system programs. At the conclusion of Chapter 1 we mentioned the automatic availability of standard subroutines, which is also part of the system facilities. The system offers extended capabilities to the user beyond those explicitly provided by the hardware. The capabilities, conventions, and restrictions defined by system programs are often referred to as *software characteristics*.

To recapitulate: The binary system of arithmetic is inherent in the hardware; existing software, however, allows the average user to ignore the binary nature of the machine and to use the decimal system in programs. With these distinctions in mind, it is nevertheless valuable for us to examine further the various types of binary coding used in computer processing.

8. *Binary Representation of Real Numbers*

As we have seen, a 32-bit word can represent an integer larger than two billion. The representation we have discussed can also be used for non-integers (or *real* numbers), simply by assuming the decimal point to be elsewhere than at the right of the word. This presents problems, however. For one thing, we must deal not with a decimal point but a binary point. In all our arithmetic instructions we would have to bear in mind the position of the points, allowing for shifting numbers to line up the point, computing its position after multiplication, and so forth. All of this can be done, but awkwardly.

There is another form of numeric representation that eliminates this problem and introduces other advantages as well. In computer terminology it is known as *floating-point* representation, and it is based on a method of expressing numbers that is very common in the sciences.

The decimal number:

$$.0000000273$$

can be written:

$$.273 \times 10^{-7}$$

while the number

$$273,000,000,000$$

can be written:

$$.273 \times 10^{12}$$

This notation has several advantages. It is obviously more compact, and often easier to read. It also simplifies arithmetic. For example, to multiply

$$.2 \times 10^{-8}$$

by $\quad .3 \times 10^6$

one multiplies the fractions (.2 by .3) and *adds* the exponents (-8 and 6) as follows:

$$(.2 \times 10^{-8}) \times (.3 \times 10^6) = .06 \times 10^{-2} = .6 \times 10^{-3}$$

Another advantage of this notation is that it allows us to distinguish *magnitude* from *precision*. Magnitude tells us how big a number is, while precision indicates how accurately something is measured. If, for example, we write

$$273,000,000,000$$

the twelve digits not only tell how big the number is, but also imply twelve-digit precision: that is, that we mean *exactly* 273 billion, and not 273 billion and two. It is more likely that most of those zeros are just place-holders required to express the magnitude in a positional system. If we write

$$.273 \times 10^{12}$$

on the other hand, we make it clear that the number has only three digits of precision. We could write

$$.27300 \times 10^{12}$$

to indicate that some of the zeros are genuine.

In the 360, numbers can be represented in this exponential or floating-point form. In brief: a 32-bit word is divided into several parts, or *fields*. The left-most bit is used again for the sign field. The next seven bits are used for the exponent, and bits 8-31 are used for the fraction. It is as if we write in decimal:

$$+ \quad 12 \quad 273$$

to represent

$$.273 \times 10^{12}$$

The number in bits 8-31 has an assumed binary point on the *left*.

There are two additional complications to 360 floating-point notation. First, the exponent in bits 1-7 is a *hexadecimal* exponent. That is, the number in bits 8-31 is to be multiplied by sixteen raised to the power of the exponent. Second, the exponent must have a sign, as well as the fraction. In decimal notation we can have

$$.273 \times 10^{12}$$
$$-.273 \times 10^{12}$$
$$.273 \times 10^{-12}$$
$$-.273 \times 10^{-12}$$

so we need two signs for this notation. The exponent in bits 1-7 must include the second sign. This could be done by reserving bit 1 for the sign of the exponent and expressing the exponent in bits 2-7. In fact, the method used in the 360 is a different one, but the difference is unimportant in the present context and need not concern us here.

Let's just look at the range of numbers that could be expressed with a fraction in bits 8-31 (24 bits) and a signed exponent in bits 1-7. Since the fraction in bits 8-31 has an assumed binary point on the left, it is always less than 1; what tells us about the *magnitude* of the number is the exponent. If bit 1 were reserved for the sign of the exponent, we would have six bits left for the exponent itself. The largest number that can be expressed in six bits is

$$111111_2 = (2^6 - 1)_{10} = 63_{10}$$

So we could express exponents from -63 to +63.

If we denote the fraction by F, and remember that it is smaller than one and has a sign associated with it, we can see that the smallest *positive* number we can express in the format under consideration would be

$$F \times 16^{-63}$$

77

while the largest positive number would be

$$F \times 16^{63}$$

A similar range holds for negative numbers. The quantity 16^{63} is roughly equivalent to 10^{75}. If you wrote a one with 75 zeros after it, that would be the rough decimal equivalent of 16^{63}; a decimal point, followed by 74 zeros, followed by a 1 is roughly equivalent to 16^{-63}.

This is essentially the range of magnitudes available in 360 floating-point notation, even though the exponent is not expressed in quite the way we describe. Clearly another advantage to floating-point notation is that it greatly increases the range of expressible magnitudes.

The 360 instructions for performing arithmetic on numbers of this type must of course be different from those for integers as described in Section 6. The 360 floating-point hardware instructions provide for handling numbers in floating-point format. This instruction set -- add, subtract, multiply, etc. -- is distinct from the corresponding integer or fixed-point instruction set.

9. *Binary Representation of Alphabetic Characters*

There are many reasons for wanting to store alphabetic characters, as well as numbers, in the computer memory, and for wanting means of manipulating these characters. We have seen two reasons for such a facility already. First, although the programs developed in Chapters 1 and 2 were designed for numeric problems, we found it convenient to instruct the computer to print titles and column headings that consisted of English text. Such text must be introduced into the computer memory, along with instructions for printing it at appropriate times.

The second instance of text-processing that we have seen is the interpretation, by the FORTRAN translator, of statements written as strings of alphabetic and numeric characters. The translator is a program to which the FORTRAN statements are data. It must, therefore, be possible to represent alphabetic characters in a binary code, as well as to find computer operations for interpreting and manipulating them.

In setting up a code for binary representation of integers, we were concerned with the necessity for performing arithmetic operations. What should be our concern in establishing a binary code for letters? What kinds of operations will we need, and will these operations suggest a natural scheme for binary coding?

One thing we will want to do is to match characters. Suppose we want to search a character string for a particular substring. The FORTRAN translator, for example, might include instructions to scan a statement for the characters 'READ'; if they are present, this might indicate to the translator that a certain type of instruction sequence must be generated for carrying out a read operation.

Clearly we will require a matching operation, but in fact this requirement doesn't impose any restriction on the coding scheme, other than consistency. For example, if we arbitrarily code the character 'A' as '10101', and want to examine another character to determine if it is also an 'A', then all the matching operation need do is check for an exact bit-for-bit match. We could even use the arithmetic operations that have been built for integer arithmetic, subtract one binary-coded character from another, and accept them as identical characters if the result of the subtraction is zero.

A more involved procedure that we might enjoy would be that of sorting characters into some useful order. In particular, we might want it to be easy to sort into alphabetic order. In order to do this, we can adopt the following scheme: let the binary code for 'A' be such that if it is viewed as a binary *number*, it is numerically smaller than the binary code for 'B,' likewise viewed as a binary number. Let this scheme govern the assignment of codes for all the letters, with A less than B, B less than C, and so forth through the alphabet. Then if we want to alphabetize a group of binary-coded characters, we can again use arithmetic operations. Subtract the first 'letter' from the second; if the result is negative, then the first 'letter' is higher in the alphabet than the second.

We could, then, code the alphabet by making the binary representation of 'A' identical to the binary integer 1, 'B' identical to the binary representation of 2, and so forth up to 26. This kind of scheme determines what is called a *collating sequence*, that is, the numeric order of the binary codes for alphabetic characters.

The code normally used in the 360 does not equate 'A' to 1, 'B' to 2, and 'Z' to 26, but it does respect the natural collating sequence. The normal code of 360 machines is called EBCDIC (for Extended Binary-Coded-Decimal Interchange Code; sometimes pronounced 'eb-see-dick'). A byte (eight bits) is used to represent a character. Eight bits allow 256 patterns, which is clearly more than the 26 required for the alphabet. But this code allows for: both upper and lower case characters; many punctuation characters; special symbols like '$', '@', '<', and so forth; representation of the numerals 0 through 9, treated as characters rather than numbers; the 'blank' or 'space', treated as a character; and some unassigned codes available for individual special requirements. As a sample of EBCDIC, the following table shows the lower-case alphabet.

Letter	*EBCDIC Binary Code*	*Letter*	*EBCDIC Binary Code*
a	1000 0001	n	1001 0101
b	1000 0010	o	1001 0110
c	1000 0011	p	1001 0111
d	1000 0100	q	1001 1000
e	1000 0101	r	1001 1001
f	1000 0110	s	1010 0010
g	1000 0111	t	1010 0011
h	1000 1000	u	1010 0100
i	1000 1001	v	1010 0101
j	1001 0001	w	1010 0110
k	1001 0010	x	1010 0111
l	1001 0011	y	1010 1000
m	1001 0100	z	1010 1001

EXERCISES

3.14   Interpreted as an EBCDIC character string, what does the following 4-byte 360 word represent?

   10001000 10000101 10010011 10010111

3.15   How would the word 'if' be coded in EBCDIC?

Check your answers before going on.

10. *Binary Instruction Code and Related Topics*

The last code that we will briefly examine is the internal instruction code. Back in Chapter 1 (Section 7) we talked about several kinds of instruction codes and programming languages. The computation of a value of a variable d by the formula

$$d = (e + s)/2$$

was represented by the FORTRAN statement:

$$D = (E + S)/2$$

If we attempt to describe precisely how this computation is carried out by hand, we see that several steps are involved. The FORTRAN statement represents a sequence of operations that must be carried out by the computer. These operations were illustrated, in Chapter 1, by the following sequence of *symbolic machine language* instructions:

Symbolic Code		*Paraphrase*
LE	4,E	'Load' register 4 with the value of e.
AE	4,S	Add to it the value of s.
HER	4,4	Halve the sum in register 4.
STE	4,D	Store it as the value of d.

where 'register 4' is one of the special CPU registers used in arithmetic operations.

Symbolic machine language must be translated into internal machine language before the instructions can be executed by the computer. But the translation is done by the computer itself. The translator is a computer program which, in effect, creates programs. A program that translates symbolic machine language is called an *assembler*. Given the sequence of instructions above, the assembler will generate *internal machine language* instructions that might, as we saw in Chapter 1, look like this:

Instruction	Paraphrase
78 4 0 F02A	Get the number at location F02A and put it in register 4 (*e*).
7A 4 0 F02E	Add to what's in register 4 the number at location F02E (*s*).
34 4 4	Divide what's in register 4 in half, and put the result in register 4.
70 4 0 F032	Store what's in register 4 into memory at location F032 (*d*).

The assembler will have performed three significant tasks. First, it will have chosen memory locations where the values of *e*, *s*, and *d* will be stored. In other words, the translator permits the expression "get me the value of E" to stand for "get me the information stored at memory location F02A". Second, the assembler will have assigned other memory locations to the instructions themselves. Third, it will have translated the individual instructions into 'internal machine code.'

But, as you may have guessed, the instruction

78 4 0 F02A

isn't *really* internal machine code, either. In order to get as close as possible to what's in the machine we need to see instructions broken down into a binary code. The instruction above is written in a code, called *hexadecimal*, that allows us an abbreviated way of specifying a binary code. The same instruction in its binary representation would be:

01111000 01000000 11110000 00101010

That's about as far as we can go. That 360 instruction, 32 bits or 4 bytes long, will occupy four memory registers. If you think of the four registers as consisting of 32 magnetic cores, and the ones and zeros as showing magnetization in one direction or another, you're close enough to seeing what's inside the computer -- and much closer than you usually need to be.

It is sometimes important, however, to illustrate exactly how information is stored in memory. The binary code is hard to read and tedious to write; the purpose of the hexadecimal code is to show the same information in more compact form. In hexadecimal code, each group of *four* bits -- half a byte -- is represented by a single character. As we know, there are sixteen different possible configurations of four bits; so we need sixteen different characters for a complete representation. Here is the key to the hexadecimal code:

Hexadecimal	*Binary*	*Hexadecimal*	*Binary*
0	0000	8	1000
1	0001	9	1001
2	0010	A	1010
3	0011	B	1011
4	0100	C	1100
5	0101	D	1101
6	0110	E	1110
7	0111	F	1111

You can go back now and compare the instruction, shown above in binary, with its hexadecimal representation.

The hexadecimal number system was introduced in Exercise 3.9. It is a number system with base sixteen. It is of particular interest for the 360 because of the correspondence between a hexadecimal digit and four binary digits. Hexadecimal can be used either as a *bona fide* number system or as a shorthand way of describing binary configurations.

EXERCISES

3.16 Here is a 32-bit configuration. Assume it represents the contents of four adjacent 360 memory registers:

       10010010   10001001   10100010   10100010

Rewrite this word in hexadecimal code.

3.17 Interpreted as an EBCDIC code, what does this word represent? (Use the table in Section 9.)

3.18 Since the word can be represented, succinctly enough, in the EBCDIC code, why do you think we would ever need to use hexadecimal? (This is not an easy question. Think about it for a while before looking at the answer.)

Check your answers before going on.

3.19   If the 32 bits of Exercise 3.16 are interpreted as an instruction, they correspond to the following symbolic machine language instruction:

        MVI   FLAG,C'I'

which can be paraphrased: Move the Character 'I' into the memory location assigned to the variable called FLAG.

   How can you determine whether the word in question should be interpreted as this instruction or as the EBCDIC word 'kiss'?

3.20   How else might the word in question be interpreted?

Check your answers before going on.

CHAPTER 4

THE COMMUNICATION OF INFORMATION

1. *Input and Output of Information*

Stated fairly generally, what a computer program does is to accept information, called 'input information'; to carry out a sequence of operations that rearrange or transform the information in some well-defined way; and to put forth the new or restructured information that results. These three stages of computer problem-solving can be called *input, processing,* and *output*. In a more anthropomorphic mood, we might call them reading (or listening), thinking, and writing (or talking.)

The FORTRAN programs developed in Chapter 2 illustrate the general flow of information processing. Each includes one or more READ statements that allow the input of raw data; each has a sequence of statements that describe operations to be performed on what has been read; and each has one or more PRINT statements that illustrate the output of results. In addition to the program that reads, computes, and prints, however, there must be two other elements: the actual input information, in some form that the computer program can accept; and the actual output information, in some acceptable form. The acceptable form for the output information depends on whether it must be acceptable to a human being or to another computer program.

A program, then, generally has input information and output information associated with it. A program plus its input data and its output data can be termed a *job*. Figure 4.1 shows the flow of a typical FORTRAN job and of the two examples from Chapter 2. Since FORTRAN is a language designed primarily for the expression of algebraic formulas, the information processing performed by FORTRAN programs is typically arithmetic.

The output of the FORTRAN programs in Figure 4.1 is generally intended for a human reader. Figure 4.2 shows a program of which the output must be acceptable to a computer program. The subroutine SQRT, which was described in Chapter 2, accepts as input a quantity transmitted to it by a program (the Atalanta-

Behemoth program, for example). After computing the square root of this program, SQRT transmits its output back to the program that asked for it.

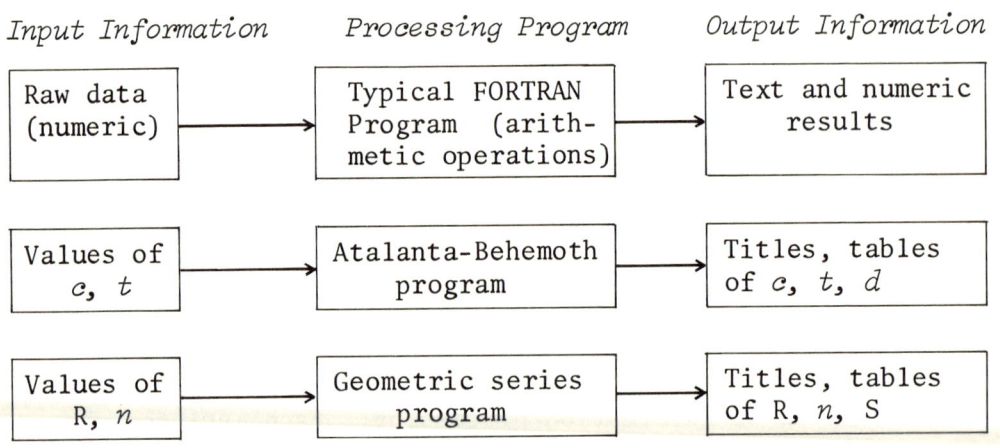

Figure 4.1

There are many other types of processing -- other than arithmetic -- that can be done by computer. For example, there are computer languages that lend themselves to problems involving the manipulation of text. A common instance is the creation by computer of various types of indexes and concordances to works of literature. The existence of a code for alphabetic characters, such as the EBCDIC code described in Chapter 3, and

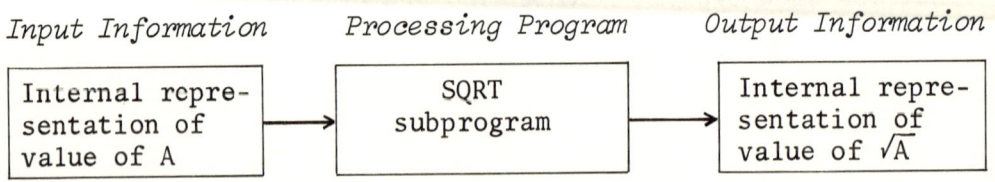

Figure 4.2

of computer instructions that manipulate this code, makes such computer applications possible. Figure 4.3 shows the structure of a job of this type. The output of the job might be a printed concordance ready for reproduction.

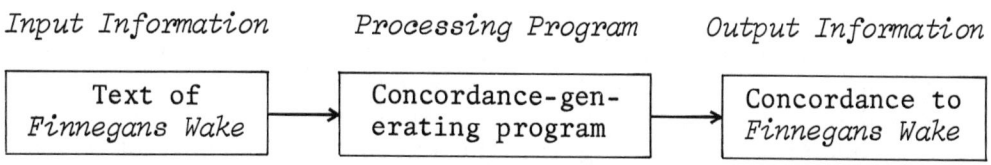

Figure 4.3

A very important instance of non-arithmetic processing is the automatic translation of FORTRAN programs into computer-executable instruction code. The FORTRAN translator (or *compiler*) is a computer program that accepts as input a set of FORTRAN statements. These statements provide a symbolic description of the program and are called a *source program*; the compiler uses this description to create an actual, executable program of computer instructions, called an *object program*. The translation is diagrammed at the top of Figure 4.4.

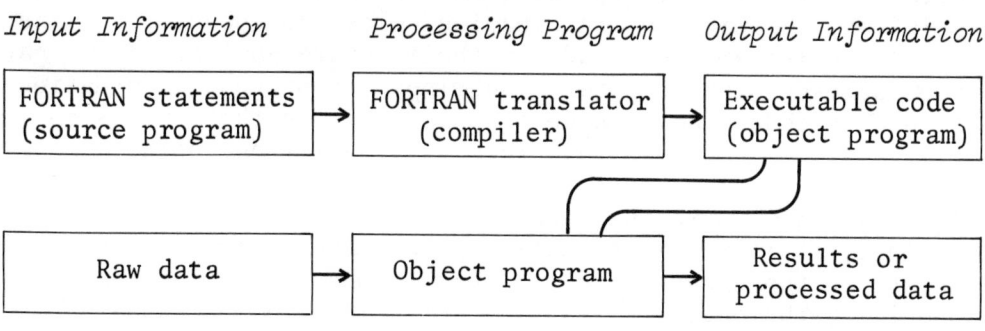

Figure 4.4

The output of this job, the object program, need not be comprehensible to a human being. It will perhaps be stored in binary form in computer memory, and the computer can then stop executing the FORTRAN compiler and begin executing the object program. At the same time, the output of the compiler may include the object program in the form of a card deck, if the user requests that such a deck be generated. The deck can be saved, and if it should be desirable to run the program again -- perhaps many times -- this *object deck* may be used. By using it, instead of the source deck, one avoids unnecessarily repeating the translation step. Again, the object deck is suitable as computer input, and not suitable for human comprehension.

A FORTRAN program involves at least two steps, as shown in Figure 4.4: the source program must be translated, and the resulting object program must be executed. This is only one example of a computer process consisting of more than one *job step*, where the output of a particular step may not be a final product. In general, *multistep* jobs have a structure such that the output of one step is the input to a later one.

The input and output information of a subprogram like SQRT may be entirely within the memory of the computer; furthermore, a particular step of a multistep job may get its input from an earlier step in a form unseen by human eyes, and may transmit output to a subsequent step in equally esoteric form. Nevertheless, at the beginning and the end of a complex computer solution, the original information comes from people, and the final results are destined for their comprehension. As we have seen already, the computer is equipped to process information in binary code. How can we take information that exists in some humanly comprehensible form -- handwritten characters, for example -- and turn it into acceptable computer input? Conversely, how can we make the computer output intelligible to people? In fact, it is not just that computer information is binary; it exists in the computer in the form of magnetic polarizations. Special techniques are required for communicating this information.

Many of the most challenging problems of computer technology lie in the area of man-machine communication. Devices for effecting this communication, known as *input/output devices*, are crucial to any computing system. Input/output devices are also used for transmitting information from one computer to another or from one program to another. An input/output device is one that permits information to be transmitted between computer memory and another medium for the storage of information.

2. *Information-Storage Media: Printing and Punched Cards*

From the computer user's point of view, the most common form of computer *output* is the printed page. Figures 4.5 and 4.6 show examples of printed output. What is printed is some body of information stored in the computer in binary form; the way it is printed is controlled by a program.

For *input*, information is most often first entered into the computer by means of some keyboard device. Using something like a typewriter, for example, you can type FORTRAN statements; each key that you hit causes signals to be sent to the computer so that the corresponding EBCDIC character is stored in memory. The typewriter-like device is connected to the computer by cables that transmit signals.

A more common method, however, is to record the information on punched cards. This is done by using a *keypunch*, a machine that also has a keyboard. Striking a key causes the machine to punch holes in the card. The keypunch is not connected to the computer. When all the information is punched on cards, the cards can then be put into a special *card reader*, a machine connected to the computer as an input device. An advantage that this method may offer over the typewriter is that the cards provide a kind of intermediate storage for the information. A FORTRAN program, for example, may be used more than once; therefore it must be entered into the computer more than once. If it is 'stored' on punched cards, then the manual keying process need not be repeated. Making minor changes or correcting errors in the program requires repunching only a few cards.

Information is recorded on a punched card in the form of small rectangular holes punched in certain locations on a standard-sized card (see Figure 4.7.) A code, sometimes called

This is an example of computer output. Information stored in the memory of an IBM 360 consisted, in this case, of the EBCDIC codes for these letters. Appropriate instructions in the 360 caused the information to be printed on an input/output device that resembles an ordinary typewriter. For each of the eight-bit EBCDIC characters in memory, the corresponding character was automatically struck by the typewriter on the page.

The typewriter can also be used for input, in which case the keys are struck by a human typist. When it is used for output the keys are not struck at all; electronic impulses directed from the computer to the typewriter cause the printing element to strike the page. The first time you watch this, it looks pretty ghostly.

Figure 4.5

ANOTHER SAMPLE OF COMPUTER OUTPUT, THIS WAS PRINTED BY AN OUTPUT DEVICE CALLED A HIGH-SPEED PRINTER. THE SPEED OF THESE PRINTERS DEPENDS ON SEVERAL FACTORS; 1000 LINES PER MINUTE IS A REASONABLE ESTIMATE OF THE SPEED WITH WHICH THIS PARTICULAR TEXT WAS DONE.

BY RELATIVELY EASY PROGRAMMING, IT IS POSSIBLE TO DO VERY FANCY THINGS WITH A HIGH-SPEED PRINTER. BELOW IS AN EXAMPLE OF HOW ONE COULD PRINT A 'LINE' GRAPH. SOPHISTICATED PICTURES CAN BE PRODUCED IN A SIMILAR MANNER. COMPUTER-GENERATED PIN-UP GIRLS ARE NOT A RARITY.

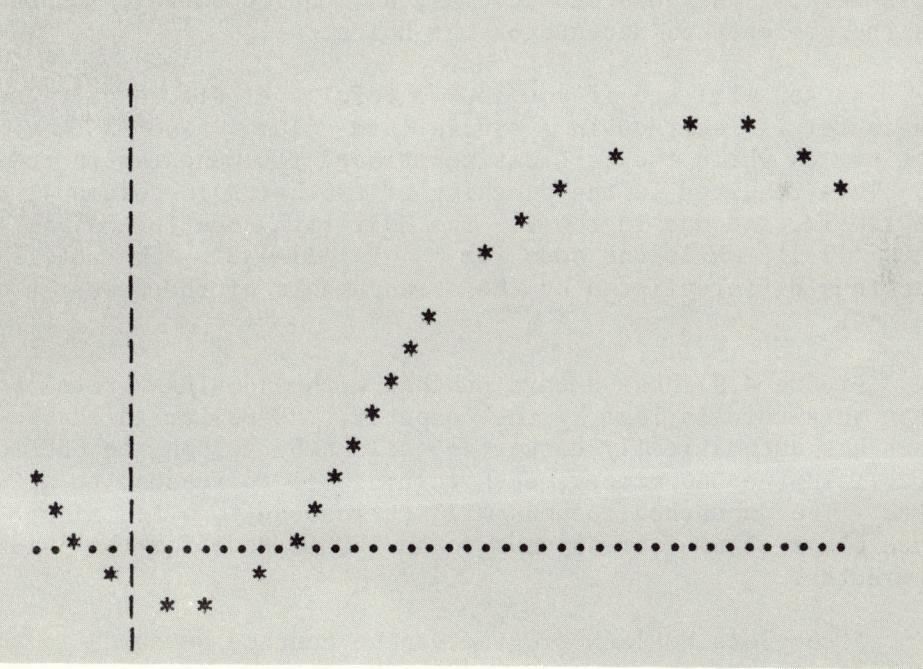

Figure 4.6

Hollerith code, is used to represent the desired characters. It is yet another binary code, since the basic unit of information is the presence or absence of a hole in a particular place. The card has eighty columns and twelve rows. The top row is called the 12-row or plus-row, the next one down is the 11-row or minus-row. These rows are unmarked on the card in Figure 4.7. The remaining ten rows are designated by the numbers 0 through 9, as marked on the card. The top of the card is called the 12-edge, the bottom is called the 9-edge.

Figure 4.8 shows a card punched in Hollerith code by means of a keypunch machine. Along the top, above the 12-row, the characters are printed as they are punched. The printing is produced by the keypunch machine for the benefit of the user; it is not recognized by the card reader when the cards are read into the computer. Neither does the computer care about any of the other printing on the card -- specifically, the little numbers marking the rows and columns; all the computer cares about is the presence or absence of the holes.

As you will see if you look carefully at Figure 4.8, each character is recorded in a single card column. The 'A' key was struck while the card was positioned for punching in column 4. This resulted in the punching of two holes in column 4, one in row 12, and one in row 1. The Hollerith code for 'A' is thus '12-1', while the code for '*' is '11-4-8'. Characters are thus differentiated by the arrangements of the holes in a column.

Figure 4.9 shows a card punched with a FORTRAN statement. When this card is read by the computer, the Hollerith characters are automatically converted, column by column, to EBCDIC code. In the 360 memory, each column will correspond to a byte. The unpunched columns will correspond to bytes also; each blank column corresponds to an EBCDIC code for the 'blank' character.

A complete FORTRAN program can be punched on cards in this fashion, one statement per card, with the order of cards the same as the order of the FORTRAN statements (which, you will remember from Chapter 2, is extremely important). The deck of cards can then be read into the computer. The information

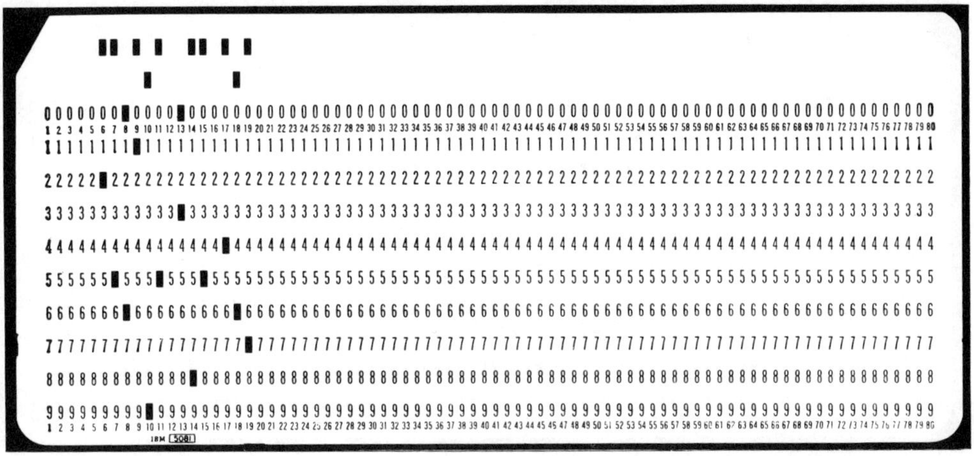

Figure 4.7

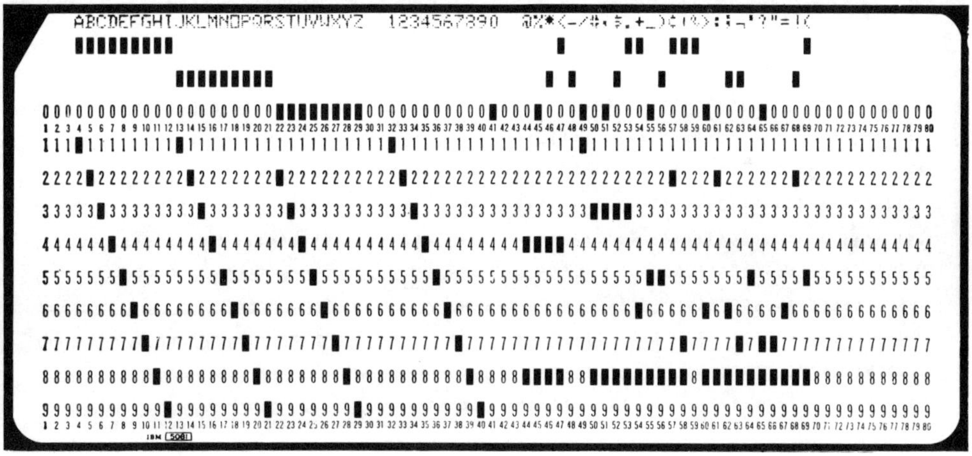

Figure 4.8

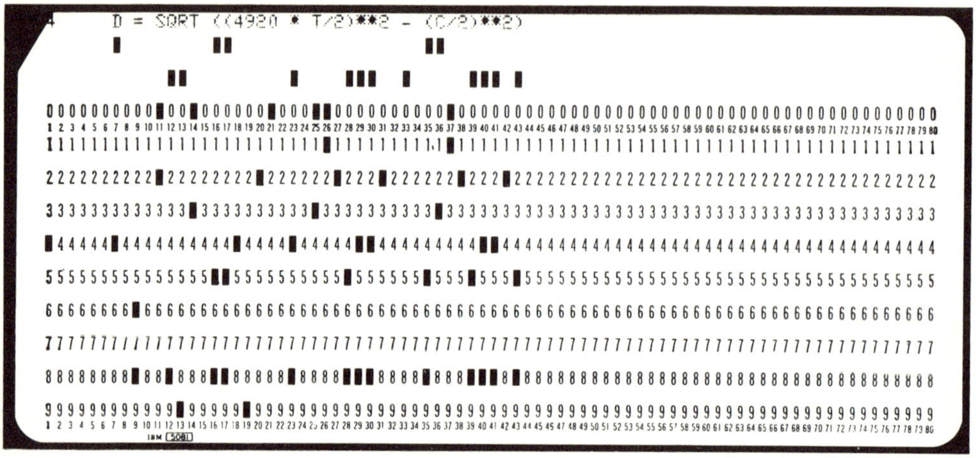

Figure 4.9

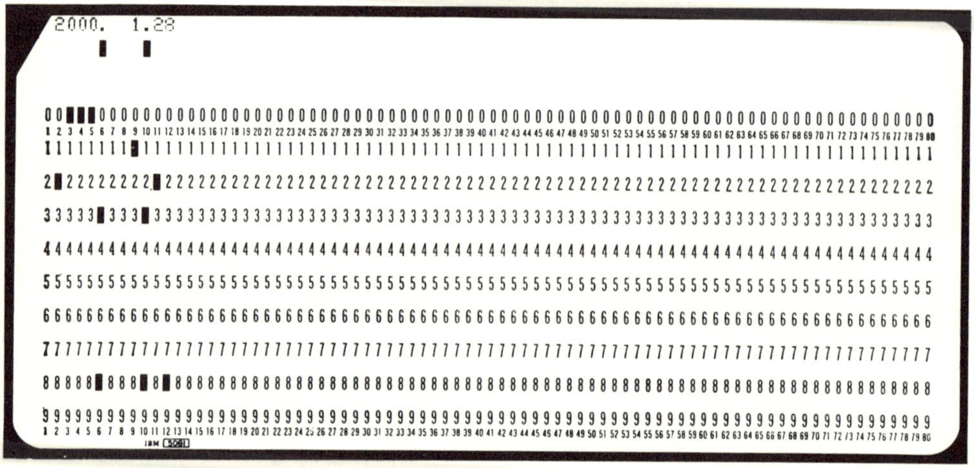

Figure 4.10

on these cards serves as input to the FORTRAN compiler. The
compiler 'reads' the cards, one at a time, and interprets the
information that they contain. It then creates an object program which will perform in the manner specified by the FORTRAN
source statements.

Frequently this translation process is followed by execution of the resulting object program; that is, when the compiler
is finished, it turns control of the computer over to the object
program. (It is not really so simple as that, as we shall see
later, but the net effect is the same.) If the object program
is derived from the Atalanta-Behemoth problem of Chapter 2, one
of the first things it does when it gets control is to 'read' a
set of numeric values for the variables C and T. Therefore it
is necessary to provide these numbers; they can be punched on a
card as shown in Figure 4.10. The Atalanta-Behemoth program
was set up, in fact, to read a card, carry out computations on
the set of data provided on the card, print results, and then
go back, *via* a program loop, to read another card with a new
set of data. It will terminate this loop when it encounters a
data card with a value of zero for C.

The punched cards containing input values for C and T, including the final one that specifies C equal to zero, can be
added on at the end of the deck of FORTRAN statements (see
Figure 4.11). When, at first, the FORTRAN compiler is in control, it will read cards from the card reader and assume them
to be FORTRAN statements. As it reads it scans the cards to
see what type of statement is punched on each. In particular,
it will look for a statement of the type

END

which should be the last statement of a FORTRAN program. When
the compiler finds this card, it stops reading cards from the
reader. The remaining cards (containing the input data) will
now just sit in the reader. Thus, when the object program is
given control, and it reads a card, the first card it gets from
the reader will be the first data card. (Again, as we shall see
later, this is a simplified description; most real computer systems are made more complex in the interests of flexibility and
efficiency.)

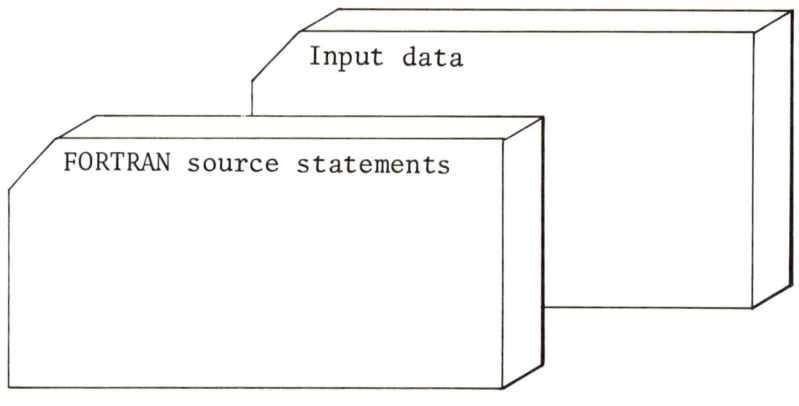

Figure 4.11

One point needs to be made about the reading of input data by the object program. The conversion of information from one type of representation, or code, to another code is an important aspect of computer systems. It was pointed out in Chapter 3 that in the 360, arithmetic operations are usually performed on numbers in binary integer or hexadecimal 'floating-point' representation. Assuming that the object program uses floating-point arithmetic, there must be a conversion from the card-coded number

$$1.28$$

and the proper internal floating-point code.

This conversion typically takes place in two steps. The first step is conversion from card code to internal EBCDIC code: one column into one byte. This conversion is accomplished by *hardware*, in this instance by the circuitry of the card reader. The second step converts the number from EBCDIC (which represents the number as a string of characters) to floating-point form. This conversion is accomplished by *software*, in the following way. The object program reads a card, and thereby gets a string of 80 EBCDIC characters; it then calls upon one of the *system subprograms* that are available to FORTRAN object programs. (These system subprograms were first described in Chapter 1, Section 8.) This subprogram is in memory just for the purpose of converting numbers that have been read from cards into the proper internal format. When it has done so, it returns control to our object program, at the same time handing over the converted number.

In general, input and output of information will involve some kind of code conversion. Often, as in the case described above, there will be two stages of conversion. Available hardware will do a preliminary conversion to a common internal code, such as EBCDIC; conversion from this to virtually any other consistent internal code is performed by programming. The second stage is performed by software, rather than hardware, because software is flexible: we need the facility for converting to a wide range of different coding schemes.

By now you should be getting a sense of the complexity of a computer system. Writing a FORTRAN program was a fairly simple matter; punching it on cards is simple too. But as a consequence of what seems so elementary, we have set in motion (on paper, at least) a surprising number of interrelated activities: the computer has been augmented by more hardware, which reads cards and prints characters; a lot of programming done by other people -- a compiler, a square-root program, a data-conversion program -- is revealed as lurking beneath the calm surface of a FORTRAN source program. There is more yet to be revealed later on in this chapter. First, however, we must take a look at other input/output devices and storage media.

EXERCISES

4.1   What is the message recorded on the punched card in Figure 4.7? (Use Figure 4.8 to find out.)

4.2   On the following pages (Figures 4.12 and 4.13,) the two programs developed in Chapter 2 have been recorded on special forms, called *coding sheets*, which are often used to prepare information for keypunching. For each of the two jobs, there are three kinds of information specified:

    (a) FORTRAN statements comprising the source program;
    (b) input data, with one set of data on each card;
    (c) additional information, called 'control statements,' identified by a slash (/) in column 1. The function of these control statements will be discussed later.

Appendix I describes the operation of one kind of keypunch machine (IBM Model 029). If you have access to a machine of this type, you can learn to use it by following the instructions in Appendix I. If you have access to a different model or kind of keypunch, or to a keyboard input device of some other type, these instructions may still be helpful. They can be used in conjunction with auxiliary information provided by your instructor or colleagues.

Because it is difficult to distinguish between the letter 'oh' and the numeral zero, the statements on the following coding sheets are written according to the convention that the letter 'oh' is written with a slash through it: 'Ø'. The slash is not part of the character to be punched; when you see 'Ø' punch 'oh,' and when you see '0' punch 'zero.'

If suitable equipment is available, use it to create the two job decks specified in Figures 4.12 and 4.13.

```
C FOR COMMENT
STATEMENT NUMBER | Cont. | FORTRAN STATEMENT
1    5 6 7   10   15   20   25   30   35   40   45   50   55   60   65

//  EXEC  FØRTHCLG,PARM.FØRT='LIST,DECK',PARM.LKED='MAP'
//FØRT.SYSIN DD *
1     PRINT 7
2     READ 8, C, T
3     IF (C .EQ. 0) STØP
4     D = SQRT ((4920 * T/2)**2 - (C/2)**2)
5     PRINT 9, C, T, D
6     GØ TØ 2
7     FØRMAT ('1     ATALANTA - BEHEMØTH DEPTH CALCULATIØNS'//
     .' RANGE (FEET)        ECHØ (SECØNDS)       DEPTH (FEET)'//)
8     FØRMAT (F6.0,F6.2)
9     FØRMAT (T4,F6.0,T26,F4.2,T42,F6.0)
      END
/*
//GØ.SYSIN DD *
 1000.   5.00
 5000.   5.00
 2000.   1.28
   0.0
/*
```

Figure 4.12

C FOR COMMENT

STATEMENT NUMBER	Cont.	FORTRAN STATEMENT

```
//  EXEC  FØRTHCLG
//FØRT.SYSIN DD *
      PRINT 13
2     READ 14,R,N
      IF (R .EQ. 0) STØP
      T=1
      S=0
      I=1
7     T=T*R
      S=S+T
      I=I+1
      IF (I .LE. N) GØ TØ 7
      PRINT 15,R,N,S
      GØ TØ 2
13    FØRMAT ('1      GEØMETRIC SERIES'//
     .'     BASE     NØ. TERMS       SUM'//)
14    FØRMAT (F5.2,I5)
15    FØRMAT (F7.2,I9,6X,F11.8)
      END
/*
//GØ.SYSIN DD *
0.5   10
0.5   20
0.5   30
0.9   30
0.9   40
0.9   50
0.0
/*
```

Figure 4.13

3. *Information-Storage Media: Magnetic Tape*

In designing or selecting storage media and devices, there are two major divergent objectives (we ignore here the questions of cost): to maximize the efficiency of computer operations, and to maximize the comfort and convenience of the user. Much of the complexity of modern computing systems is a result of efforts to maximize both these virtues. In the past, major efforts of technological development were devoted to high-speed input/output devices and computing systems that aimed at getting the most work out of the computer. Recent years have shown not a reversal but a shift of interest; major efforts are now being devoted to making the computer more and more accessible to non-specialist users, without unduly degrading the efficiency of the machines.

Devices that maximize the efficiency of computer operations are characterized by the speed with which information can be transmitted to and from computer memory. Punched cards, although convenient in some respects, do not permit very high-speed transmission; they are also a relatively bulky way to store information. Magnetic tape is a widely used medium that provides more compact storage and higher transmission rates.

Magnetic tape is a coated plastic tape, usually one-half inch wide, wound on reels that may hold up to 2400 feet of tape. It is similar to the standard audio tape used for recording music; instead of recording continuous sound patterns, however, it records binary information. The information is recorded by magnetization of small distinct areas of the ferromagnetic coating.

The computer (under control of a program, of course) can read or write a magnetic tape that is mounted on a *tape unit* directly connected to the computer. The tape unit has a read/write head, as does an audio tape recorder. Tape can be passed across the read/write head at fairly high speeds; the tape unit is designed to permit starting and stopping of the tape at high speed without breaking of the tape.

Information may be transcribed onto tape from punched cards; a computer with a card-reader and a tape unit reads the

information from cards into memory and writes it out onto tape.
(This process is called *card-to-tape* conversion.) The tape
record corresponding to a punched card is called a *card-image*.
Conversely, the information on a tape can be read by computer
and transcribed to punched cards or to printed form (*tape-to-card* or *tape-to-print* conversion.)

Some user programs produce output on tape which is never
printed or punched (i.e., is never 'seen' by the user) but remains on tape for further processing. The tape is used as
direct input to another program. This might be the case where
a large volume of intermediate computational output is produced,
and another program -- perhaps a subsequent job step -- is designed to reduce it to more manageable form. Tape is useful
for storing large masses of raw data in compact form. It can
also be used for storing large programs (including such system
programs as the FORTRAN compiler), which are recorded on tape
rather than as bulky source or object program decks.

The capacity of magnetic tape is a function of the number
of bits that can be recorded on a cross-section of the tape,
and the number that can be recorded in a one-inch longitudinal
section (see Figure 4.14.) The bits recorded across the width
of a tape are called a tape character. Information is recorded
on seven or nine longitudinal parallel *tracks*; one of these
tracks is not used for data but is dedicated to validity-checking information. Thus tapes may have a 'data width' of six or
eight bits; stated differently, tape characters may be six or
eight bits long. Since the basic unit of 360 storage is the
eight-bit byte, most tapes used with the 360 are nine-track
tapes.

The 'recording density' of a tape is the number of characters recorded in an inch-long section of the tape (which is
identical to the number of bits per track in an inch-long section.) Current standard recording densities are 200, 556, 800,
and 1600 characters per inch (cpi). (The unit is often called
'bits per inch' [bpi], which really means 'bits per track per
inch.' The total number of *bits* recorded at 1600 cpi in a one-inch slice of nine-track tape is 12,800.)

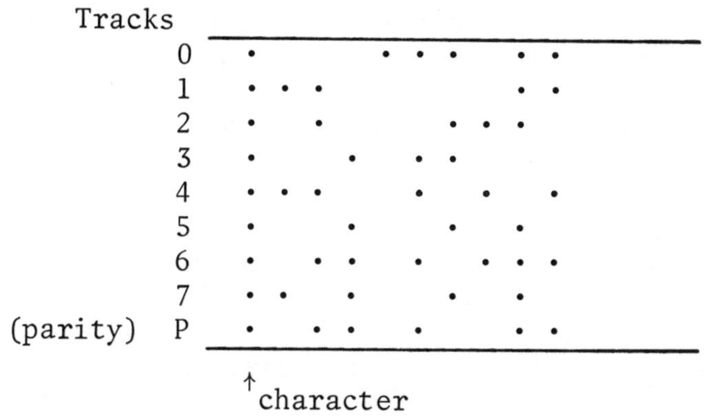

```
Tracks _____
    0     •   •  •   • •
    1    •••         • •
    2    •     •    •••
    3    •  •   ••
    4    •••    •  •  •
    5    •    •    •   •
    6    • •  • •  •
    7    ••   •      •
(parity) P ____•__•_•___•____•_•_____
              ↑
              character
```

Figure 4.14

The extra track, or 'parity track,' is used for something called 'parity checking.' It contains redundant information that helps to avoid hardware errors in reading or recording data. Suppose that the following 360 word is to be written on nine-track tape:

    10001000   10000101   10010011   10010111

As each character is written, a check is made for an odd or an even number of 'ones' in the character. If the number is even, a one is written in the parity track -- otherwise not. The characters above can be visualized on tape like this:

```
         Track  0      1 1 1 1
                1      0 0 0 0
                2      0 0 0 0
                3      0 0 1 1
                4      1 0 0 0
                5      0 1 0 1
                6      0 0 1 1
                7      0 1 1 1
       (parity) P      1 0 1 0
```

Thus every tape character *including* the parity bit has an odd number of ones. When a tape is read, if a character plus the parity bit has an even number of ones, there must be an

105

error somewhere. This condition, called a *redundancy error* or parity error, is usually the result of a transient failure in the hardware or a flaw in the tape itself. If a redundancy error is detected, provision can be made for correcting or at least diagnosing the error.

There are variations on this technique. What has just been described is called vertical, odd, parity checking. Some tapes are written with even parity, which is just a minor variation (the parity bit forces all characters to have an even number of ones.) Longitudinal parity checking involves writing an extra character at the end of a block of characters. Each bit of this character serves to check the parity of bits along a track. The combination of vertical and longitudinal parity checking provides a thorough safeguard against undetected tape errors.

Information on magnetic tape is grouped into units larger than the character or word. A tape *record* is a related group of characters or words; normally the record is the unit of reading or writing. For example, if Hollerith cards are transcribed onto tape by computer they are often transcribed so that one card goes into one tape record. Similarly, if tape is transcribed to printed form, one line of print may be produced by one tape record. The end of a record is indicated by an interval of blank tape (about 0.6 inch long) called a *record gap* or *inter-record gap*.

A related group of *records* is called a *file* (or a dataset). A file consists of one or more records followed by a record gap, a special tape mark or *end-of-file (EOF) mark*, and another record gap (see Figure 4.15). An end-of-file mark must be explicitly written on tape; during reading, it is possible for a program to test whether an end-of-file has been encountered.

As an illustration of the relationship between records and files: suppose a program is required to process two distinct groups of data in different ways, each group being comprised of a variable or indeterminate number of sets of data items. Each set of items might be a record (e.g., transcribed from one card), with the first *group* recorded as one file, and the second as another. The program would read a data record, process it, read another record, repeat the processing (using a program loop), and so forth until an end-of-file was detected. The end-of-file would indicate the end of the first group of data; the second group, to be processed by a different section of the program, would consist of the second file of card-image records.

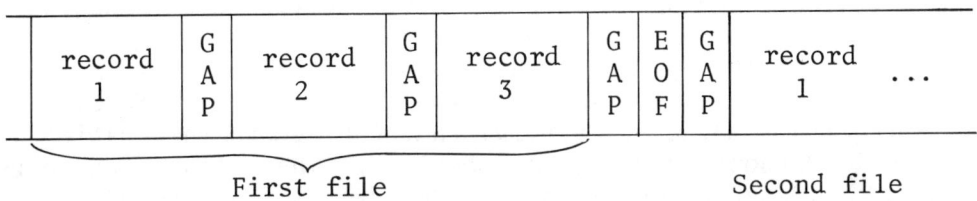

Figure 4.15

A final note about tape: a tape reel ten and a half inches in diameter, holding 2400 feet of tape, can contain information that would require on the order of half a million punched cards. This many cards would occupy roughly fifty cubic feet of storage space. They'd be heavy, too.

4. *Information-Storage Media: High-Speed Large-Capacity Devices*

Magnetic tape provides a convenient form of storage for large quantities of information. It is appropriate, at this point, to observe that some of the most important uses of the computer require that large amounts of data be available for high-speed transmission. Much of the time the value of the computer lies not so much in its 'computational' ability as in the speed with which it can search through masses of information, perhaps performing relatively trivial operations on selected items.

Examples of this type of computer application include: maintenance of personnel files, including payroll processing;

large-scale billing systems, like those used by utility companies or credit organizations; inventory control systems; library cataloguing and circulation systems (still in their infancy, but likely to be of tremendous value.) Automatic information retrieval is an application that promises to have as much impact on both research and industry as any computer technique developed so far. Information retrieval is also in its early stages, and beset by problems; one of the problems is the volume of information to be processed, which is so huge that even current high-speed large-capacity devices are inadequate.

Current storage media in general use are variations of the principle used for magnetic tape: a movable surface is coated with a magnetic material that can record information by magnetized spots at discrete locations. These spots can be recorded or detected by 'read/write heads' as the recorded surface moves past them. A rotating cylinder, for example, can have information recorded on its surface in parallel bands; as this drum rotates, each band passes under a stationary read/write head. (The principle is very like that of a music box.)

A device in wide use today is the disk-storage device, of which a schematic appears in Figure 4.16. Information is stored on the surfaces of parallel concentric rotating disks. The 'bands' here are in concentric circles on the surface of a disk. The heads can be positioned at any radius, and since the disks rotate, the entire surface is accessible.

The disk device does not suffer from the major disadvantage of magnetic tape, which should be familiar to anyone who uses a tape recorder. It is often necessary to spend a lot of time passing over magnetic tape in order to get at some piece of data in the middle or at the end. With a device like the disk -- called a 'direct-access' device -- it is possible to move directly to the place where the desired information is stored.

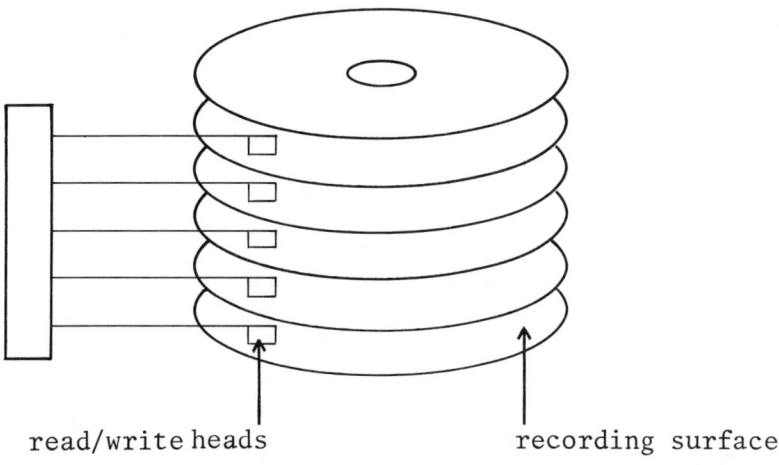

Figure 4.16

5. *Input/Output Devices for People*

As we have seen, direct-access devices, magnetic tapes, and even punched cards are examples of storage media designed to make information readily intelligible to the computer. Consequently, they are best used for efficient transfer of large quantities of information at intermediate stages of computer processing. At the beginning and the end, however, we need media at least as intelligible and useful as standard methods of communication among people. Although the punched card is still popular as the first step in communicating with the machine, it is more suited to the machine than to the man, and is therefore gradually being replaced by more convenient methods.

As illustrated by Figures 4.5 and 4.6, printed computer output is standard, and perfectly intelligible. The high-speed printer of Figure 4.6 is one of the most common of computer printing devices. For reasons of efficiency, printers of this type frequently can print only a limited number of different characters: for example, there may be only upper-case letters. On the other hand, more complete character sets can be obtained for these machines. Upper- and lower-case printers produce documents of good quality; special printing elements can be designed for foreign alphabets, technical symbols, and so forth.

High-speed printers have even been used to create Braille documents, by virtue of the fact that the type hits the page with sufficient force that a period, for example, makes a tangible indentation. This is a rather artificial application, however. There are also genuine Braille printers attached to computer systems as output devices.

For input, the typewriter described in Figure 4.5 is becoming more and more popular. The 'typewriter terminal' is connected to the computer, frequently by telephone lines, so that it can be physically far removed from the computer. A computer user can have such a remote terminal installed in his office, for example, and use it to submit programs for computer processing. When a key is struck, a signal is transmitted over the lines to the computer; this signal results in the storage, in computer memory, of the EBCDIC code for the character represented by the struck key. The same typewriter can be used for output, with the transmission process reversed. For large amounts of output the typewriter is intolerably slow, but for short messages it's pretty good. That's from *our* point of view. From the computer's point of view, the typewriter is ludicrously slow in either direction; a computer getting a message from a good typist has been compared to a man receiving a telegram at the rate of one character per day. As you will see in Chapter 5, however, there are ways to compensate for -- and even take advantage of -- the disparity between human and computer speeds.

In recent years much developmental effort has been expended on improving the computer's ability to communicate on our level; the next few years should show significant practical advances. There are 'optical character recognition' devices, which can scan printed text by optical techniques, and transmit the corresponding binary information to the computer. At present these scanners can read only special type fonts, but as they become more versatile, the range of fonts will increase. A computer will be able to 'read' an ordinary book; thus the necessity for keypunching or otherwise recoding a text will be eliminated. These optical devices can even read carefully hand-printed characters. Cursive handwriting, however, with all its idiosyncracies, is another story. Although computer recognition of handwriting is a subject of research, it is a long way from practical reality.

There is a very interesting class of I/O devices that are built around a cathode-ray-tube (CRT) screen. The screen is similar to a television screen, in that both display images composed of points of light of varying intensity. How good the image is -- or how clear -- depends on the number and density of points that make up the image. Some CRT devices display many more points per square inch than a television screen, and can project very clear, complex pictures. (Some, on the other hand, cannot.) These pictures can be created by the programmer in a variety of ways. For example, he can specify two points and indicate that a straight line or an arc is to be drawn between them. He can display alphabetic characters from a pre-designed, prestored set, or he can design his own 'type font' by specifying every point in the composition of every letter.

Some CRT devices have a built-in camera for photographing what is displayed on the screen. Computer-generated animated movies have been made using a CRT. The computer is useful for automatic 'typesetting' -- it can be programmed to do pagination, margin alignment, and so forth -- and the text can then be displayed on the CRT for photographing. A high-quality CRT can display at one time, with readable quality, as much text as appears on a page of the *New York Times*.

There are two standard ways of using a CRT device for input. One is by attaching a keyboard in such a way that when a key is struck, the corresponding character is displayed on the screen. A device like this can function as a 'remote terminal' similar to the typewriter described earlier. As you type, you watch the characters on the screen instead of on paper; at the same time, they are transmitted to the computer. When you have filled up the screen, you can erase it and start in at the top again. You do not get any 'hard copy' this way, but what you have typed is stored by the computer. If you later want to read what you have written, you can type in a request to have it displayed on the screen. Whatever will fit on the screen is displayed; when you have read it, you can ask for the next screenful.

The other way of using a CRT for input is by a device called a *light-pen*. This is a stylus-like affair containing a photocell, and attached by a cord to the terminal. It can be used to 'draw' on the screen; the computer can tell where the light-pen is pointing, and can generate an image on the screen that follows the track of the pen. A CRT terminal with a light-pen usually has a set of control buttons that direct various functions. For example: you might point with the light-pen at an image on the screen, push a button marked 'MOVE,' and then point to another part of the screen. The computer would then erase the image and regenerate it at the new position.

The use of devices like CRT's, remote terminals, and optical scanners depends on rather sophisticated programming. This programming is normally done by the computer manufacturer, the manufacturer of the I/O device, and the professional staff of the individual computer installation. The programs that they provide -- the software of the computer system -- serve both to extend the physical capabilities of the hardware components, and to mask their physical complexities. A user of the system, with a problem to be solved, should not have to be aware of the physical differences between tapes, disks, or drums. Nor should he have to know about the programming techniques required to make a straight line appear on a screen after he has sketched a wobbly one with a light-pen.

Ideally, the user should be able to sit at a remote terminal -- perhaps a very fancy one with CRT, light-pen, optical scanner, and typewriter all together -- and regard it as a tool, an extension of his own capabilities, without knowing or caring how it works. He might not know or care that it is connected to a computer, for instance. Most people use telephones and automobiles this way: the telephone as an extension of the voice, the automobile of the legs. Once the rules of operation are learned and become automatic, the mechanism or process becomes almost invisible unless it breaks down. It is pleasant to imagine the computer presenting an equally simple front to the user.

It does not, however, and to many people this is a disappointment. The reason may be that computers of the sort we are discussing are multipurpose tools. Although the telephone system is an extremely complex piece of engineering, its function is quite simple: it extends the range of your voice. It is less easy to say what kind of tool or extension the computer represents. To say that the computer is an extension of the brain surely raises more questions than it answers.

In fact, using a computer system to calculate the depth of the ocean floor is probably, more than anything else, like shopping for a particular item at Macy's. The customer is painfully aware of alternative possibilities, and at times may be overwhelmed by them. He is also very much aware, as at the department store, of the *process* of getting what he needs from a large, general-purpose system. It is to be expected, however, that in the future the computer system, if not the department store, will come to function much more smoothly. We try to increase the potential functions of the machine and at the same time to make the process more and more transparent. The development of software is guided by both these aims.

The next chapter traces the development of one kind of software: the central operating system. It is designed to be read while you are waiting for the results of the next exercise. Chapter 6 is designed to be read after you have the results.

EXERCISE 4.3

The substance of this exercise is to take the two job decks created for Exercise 4.2 and submit them to computer processing. The details of the procedure for so doing will vary from installation to installation; in a single installation they will probably vary from year to year. We present here a description of a standard procedure used at the Columbia University Computer Center. Some of the steps are strictly peculiar to that environment; others are peculiar to a class of installations that use the IBM 360. These procedures should be checked against those in use at your installation, if you have one. If you do not, perhaps reading on will give you a mental picture of what it is like.

A. *Accounting information and job identification*

Since little in this world is free, most computer centers have devised ways of accounting for the computer time used by a job and charging the user therefor. It is generally necessary for users to supply, with each job: an account number to which time will be charged; the name of the user (in case several users share the same account); an identification of the job itself (in case a user submits several jobs in a short period of time).

In these examples the account number has been omitted but is assumed to be seven characters long. The *job name* is made up of the user's initials concatenated with an identifier like ABDC (for Atalanta-Behemoth Depth Calculations) or GEOM (for geometric series).

B. *The JOB card*

The first card of a job deck is usually a control card that provides information about the job as a whole, including:

    account number
    user identification
    job identification
    estimated computer time required

and other 'administrative' information. The job card used at
Columbia is illustrated in Figure 4.17. It is distinctive in
color (cerise) and format, and thus helps the computer operators to separate decks that have been put one after another into
a card reader. The punching conforms to IBM 360 Operating System (OS/360) conventions.

   Columns 1 and 2 contain a slash; OS/360 control cards all
contain either '//' or '/*' in the first two columns. The
slashes and the characters 'JOB' in columns 12-14 tell the

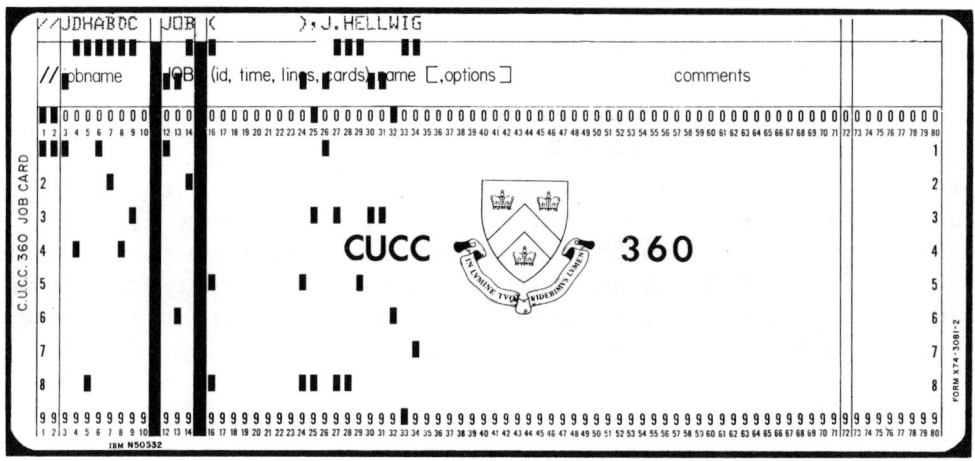

Figure 4.17

computer what kind of card this is: a card that signals the beginning of a new job and contains accounting information. The
job name starts in column 3, and it must not go past column 10.
Beginning in column 16 is punched the account number, enclosed

in parentheses, followed by a comma, followed by the programmer's name with no intervening blanks.

This card can specify, in addition:

   time: number of minutes allowed;
   lines: maximum number of printed lines expected as output;
   cards: maximum number of punched cards expected as output.

If a job is expected to run for 5 minutes, produce 10,000 lines of output and 800 punched cards, the JOB card would look like this:

   //JDHLARGE JOB (account,5,10000,800),J.HELLWIG

Most installations have local *default* estimates; that is, quantities that are assumed if none are specified. Thus the defaults applied to the job card in the illustrations might be:

   time: 1 minute
   lines: 1000
   cards: 100

Clearly, since this card is so unique to an installation, it will probably be different from what is illustrated here. You will have to punch up your own JOB card according to the conventions of your installation. If they are very close to the conventions shown here, you will at least have to put your own initials into the job name (columns 3-10), your own account number in its place (columns 17-23), and your own initial and name in place of the one illustrated.

C. *Remaining control cards*

The second card in both jobs is the first one shown in Figures 4.12 and 4.13. For job ABDC it reads:

   //   EXEC   FORTHCLG,PARM.FORT='LIST,DECK',PARM.LKED='MAP'

Note that there are no blanks from FORTHCLG all the way to the end. For GEOM it reads simply:

   //   EXEC   FORTHCLG

This card tells the computer what kind of job this is: to wit, a job that requires a FORTRAN compilation, subsequent loading of the object program along with necessary system library subprograms, followed by execution of the object program. It also supplies some optional information about how these steps are to be carried out. The first part of the information more or less stands for: *EXEC*ute the *FORT*ran version *H C*ompiler, *L*oad the object program, and *G*o, i.e., execute it. The significance of the remaining information will be discussed in Chapter 6.

The next control card,

```
//FORT.SYSIN DD *
```

tells the computer that what comes next is the source program. Never mind how -- the computer is conditioned to interpret that card that way.

What follows is, indeed, the source program. The last card of the source deck is the END statement, and it is followed by another control card:

```
/*
```

This card marks the end of the input to the compiler. It must be there because the compiler is quite willing to translate a series of FORTRAN source programs. It recognizes the end of each one by the END card, and the end of the whole batch of them by the '/*' card.

Next is a control card,

```
//GO.SYSIN DD *
```

which indicates that what comes next is input to the object program. This card is obviously similar to the one that preceded the source deck; there is some method to this madness. As you might guess, a card of the form:

```
//step.SYSIN DD *
```

is generally used to preface the input data destined for a job step named 'step.'

Next are the input data cards. For the Atalanta-Behemoth

problem, these consist of three cards, each containing a value for C (distance between ships, in feet) and a value for T (travel time of echo, in seconds). For the geometric series problem, each data card has a value for the base R, and one for N, the number of terms to be computed.

In both jobs, the input data is followed by a '/*' card, which marks the end of the input data -- and in this case, the end of the entire job.

D. *Submittal procedure*

At Columbia, as at many other installations, the job deck is preceded by a special card called the 'service request card,' which is filled out by hand. The Columbia version of this card is illustrated in Figure 4.18. It provides a medium for communication between the user and the computer operators, who keep the system running. The job deck, held together by a rubber band, is turned over to the operations staff; they carry it through a number of stages, beginning by putting it in a card reader. The eventual outcome is: some printed pages, possibly some punched cards, and the original input deck. All of these are returned to you.

If the system allows the submission of jobs through a remote terminal (as described in Section 5, above), some steps are bypassed. You may type your program at the terminal and receive the output there, too. No cards are involved at all. The information given on the control cards may be typed in the same manner, or it may be furnished in a freer format.

After checking out the local procedures at your installation, you should submit the two jobs for processing. Chapter 6 discusses the results in some detail; ideally it should be read after you have the results of both jobs. Chapter 5 may be read while you are waiting for them to be run.

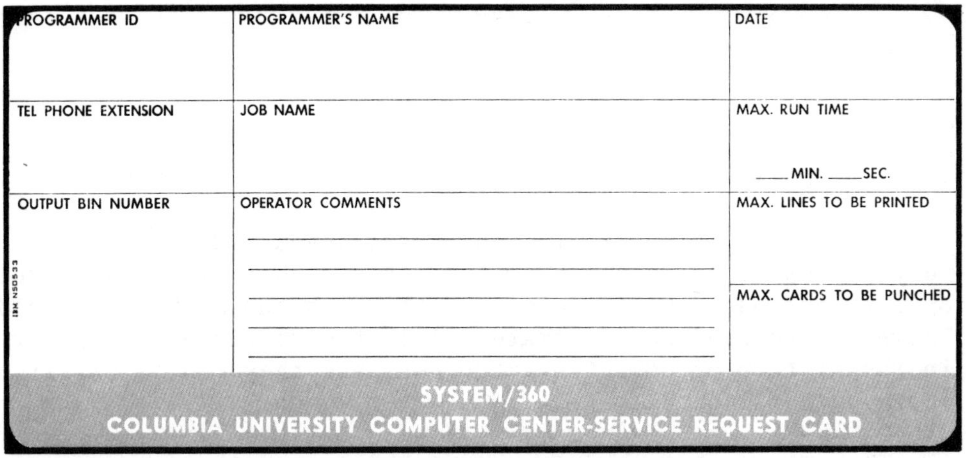

PROGRAMMER ID	PROGRAMMER'S NAME	DATE
TEL PHONE EXTENSION	JOB NAME	MAX. RUN TIME ____ MIN. ____ SEC.
OUTPUT BIN NUMBER	OPERATOR COMMENTS	MAX. LINES TO BE PRINTED
		MAX. CARDS TO BE PUNCHED

SYSTEM/360
COLUMBIA UNIVERSITY COMPUTER CENTER-SERVICE REQUEST CARD

Figure 4.18

CHAPTER 5

OPERATING SYSTEMS

1. *Programming Systems and Operating Systems Distinguished*

Since any computer of significant speed and capacity is very expensive to maintain, methods are constantly being developed to increase the efficiency with which the machine is used. There are several basic strategies that were recognized early in the history of computing machines, and they can be described roughly as follows:

1. The computer performs arithmetic and logical operations at very high speed; it is slowed down, however, during input and output of information, because it is limited by the speed of the I/O devices, which cannot keep up with the central processing unit (CPU). Any increase in the efficiency of input and output will thus increase the overall efficiency of the computer.

2. If the computer is running but idle -- for example, if it must wait, if only for a few minutes, between the conclusion of one job and the initiation of the next -- then valuable time is being lost. Idle time, especially between jobs, should be reduced to a minimum.

3. Wherever possible, the computer should perform routine administrative functions like accounting for the machine time used by a job, scheduling jobs to be run, terminating jobs that have run too long. It is desirable to reduce the number of tasks and decisions performed by the human operators of the system, as long as such tasks are straightforward enough for the computer to perform them successfully.

4. A computer system designed to increase the efficiency of the machine should not seriously decrease the efficiency of its users. A user's efficiency is decreased if he must wait an excessive amount of time before he gets back the results of his computer job, or if he must learn excessively esoteric procedures in order to get his job run.

An *operating system* is a set of programs that control the continued operation of the computer over a *long period* of time -- in particular, throughout the continuous processing of a large number of individual user jobs. This set of controlling programs is usually combined with other sets of programs called *programming systems*. A programming system is designed to make the computer more accessible to the user. In particular, the aim is to bridge the gap between the language of the machine and the natural language in which the user expresses his problems. An example of a programming system is the FORTRAN system, which includes the compiler and the library of subprograms associated with it.

A programming system functions within an operating system and is closely tied to it; it is not always easy to distinguish the parts and functions of one from another. For the remainder of this chapter, however, we will be concerned primarily with the operational aspects of computer software systems.

2. *Classic Batch-Processing*

We can begin by considering one of the earliest types of operating system, what we might call the classic batch-processing system, or 'batch-processing with off-line input and output.' This type of system was used extensively, until recent developments in hardware and software techniques made it obsolete. Since it is conceptually simpler than current systems, we will use it to introduce some basic systems concepts.

The batch-processing system that we will describe centers around a large high-speed digital computer, the IBM 7094, which is one of the so-called 'second-generation' machines. Without going into the essential differences between the generations, let us merely observe that the first generation consisted of the first general-purpose high-speed electronic digital computers; the third generation includes the IBM 360; the fourth generation is as yet unborn at the time of this writing.

Since it is desirable to speed up I/O, and since the computer can read and write magnetic tape much faster than it can read or punch cards, or print, then it makes good sense to use tape for all input and output to the 7094. We indicated earlier, however, that we need a computer to transcribe cards to tape and vice versa. The batch-processing system employs another computer, the primary function of which is to perform card-to-tape, tape-to-card, and tape-to-printer conversion.

This auxiliary computer runs independently of the 7094, and is called an *off-line* or *peripheral* computer. This scheme only makes sense if the off-line computer is much less expensive to operate than the main computer. The IBM 1401, for example, is limited in capabilities and fairly inexpensive by comparison with the 7094; it is also rather good at doing the kind of I/O required.

The relationship between the main and the peripheral computers is diagrammed in Figure 5.1. A user's job deck is put into a bin with other jobs of similar type; when the bin is full, the *batch* of jobs is put into the card reader attached to the 1401. The 1401 transcribes the card-images onto a tape. This tape, called the *batch input tape*, thus contains the card-images of job deck after job deck, in succession. This tape is then used as input to the 7094.

The 7094 is controlled by the operating system programs. These programs read the input tape and process the jobs, proceeding automatically from one job to the next. Whenever a particular job generates output that is to be punched or printed, the output is written onto a magnetic tape. This tape is called the *batch output tape*. The output of each job is written just after the output of the preceding job.

When the entire batch of jobs has been run, the operators remove the input tape and the output tape from the 7094 tape units. During the time that the batch was being processed, a new input tape was prepared at the 1401, containing the next batch. This tape is now mounted on a 7094 tape unit, and processing of the next batch begins immediately. Somebody carries the output tape of the first batch to the 1401 and mounts it on one of the 1401 tape units. The 1401 reads the output tape and transcribes its records to cards and printed lines. The punched and printed output from all the jobs in the batch is then separated, combined with the appropriate input decks, and

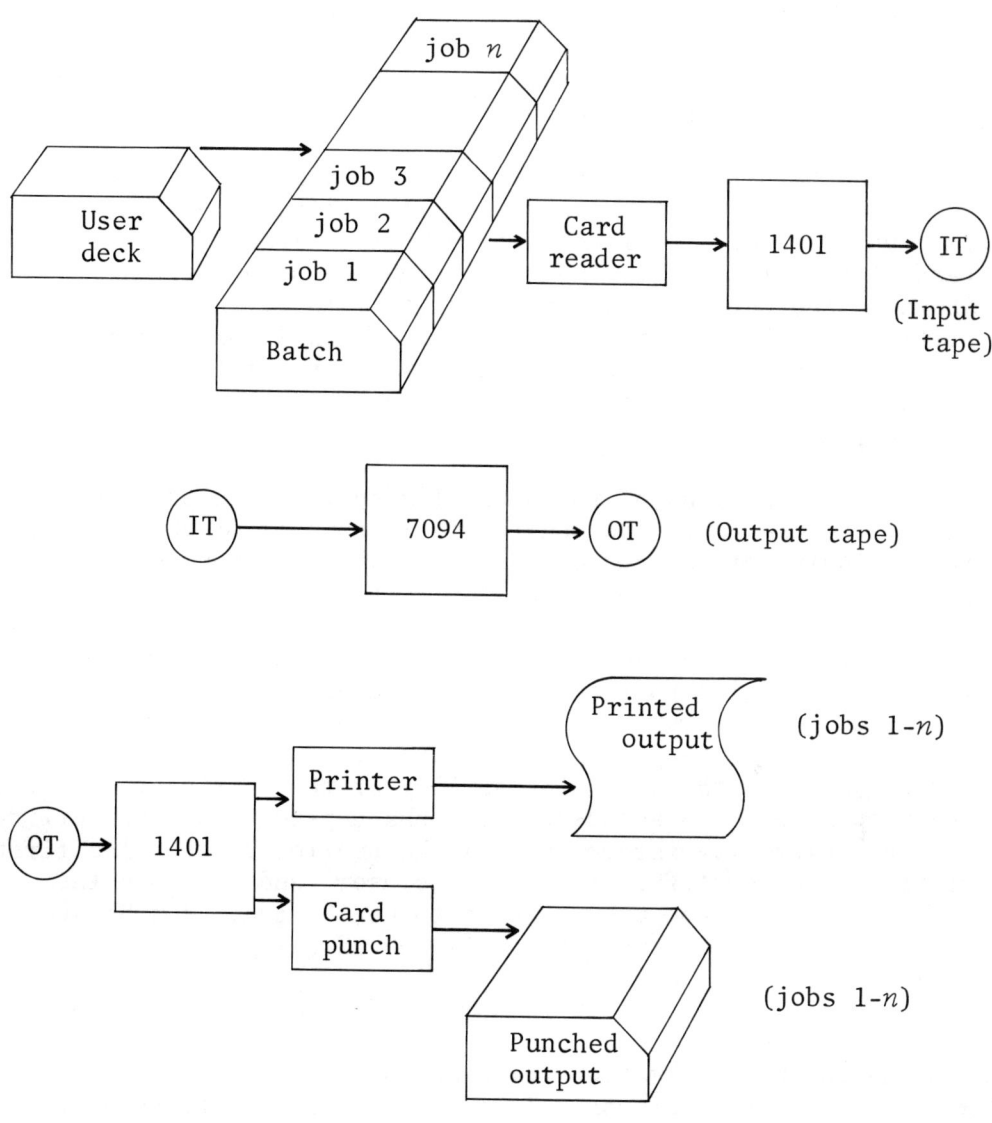

Figure 5.1

returned to the users.

Now, let's look for a moment at the format of the input tape. The 1401 has transcribed each card as a tape *record*; each job deck is written as a *file*, i.e., as a series of records terminated by an end-of-file (EOF) indicator. When a new batch is begun, the input tape is positioned on the 7094 tape unit so that the first record that is read is the first card of the first job. The output tape is positioned, on another tape unit, so that the output of the first job will be written at the beginning of the tape. When a job 'prints' a line, the information to be printed will be a record on the output tape; the output for each job will be terminated by an EOF indicator.

The key section of the operating system is a program called the *monitor*. The monitor is in control of the 7094 at the beginning of the processing of a batch. (When we speak of a program as 'in control,' we mean that its instructions are currently being executed. Many programs are usually in memory at one time, but only one is being executed at a given moment.) The monitor begins to read the card-images of the first job in the batch. The first cards encountered are *control cards*, which exist for the purpose of telling the monitor some pertinent facts about the job. The ability of the monitor to control the processing of a succession of jobs depends upon its ability to 'recognize' key information in the control cards. The first control card identifies the job, the user, and probably the account to which computer time is to be charged. A subsequent one may tell the monitor that this job is going to call on the FORTRAN compiler. A different job, by using different control cards, might indicate that the program is in a different programming language, and requires a different translator. Depending on the information furnished by the control cards, the monitor will transfer control to the appropriate translator program.

Now, many of the components of the programming and operating system are big, in terms of memory space, and they cannot all be kept in memory at once. Instead, they are kept on tape or disk or drum storage, which thus serves as an extension of the available memory space; these devices are referred to as *secondary storage*, as opposed to the *main memory* of the computer. Programs in secondary storage are brought into main memory when they are to be executed. When the monitor transfers control to the FORTRAN compiler, it cannot simply execute a transfer instruction to a location in memory, because the compiler is (probably) not there. The monitor must read the compiler program into memory from secondary storage and then transfer control to it. Parts of the monitor may be overlaid in memory; that is, the compiler may be stored on top of them. This is all right, though, because a copy of the monitor is in secondary storage, too. When the compiler is finished, and must transfer control back to the monitor, it will first cause a fresh copy of the monitor to be read into main memory.

When the compiler is given control, the monitor has read past the control cards on the input tape; thus the tape is positioned with the read-head just in front of the source program deck. When the translator executes instructions to read the input tape, the first source statement will be read. The translator reads record after record (card after card) of the source program, until it recognizes the END statement. At this point it stops reading and creates the binary object program.

By means of a control card, the user has been able to ask that the object program be punched onto cards as an object deck; he may also have asked that it be brought into memory and executed as a subsequent step in his job. Let us assume that he asked for both deck and execution; the binary object program will in this case be written in two places. It will be written on the output tape for later off-line punching; thus the first file on the output tape may be the object deck for the first job in the batch. It will also be written onto another tape, called the *load tape*, in a form suitable for subsequent 'loading' into memory.

Figure 5.2 diagrams the flow of a batch-processing system. The input tape is represented on the left, the output and load tapes on the right. In the center is a diagram of the flow of control among parts of the system, with the horizontal arrows roughly indicating the relative positions of the tapes while each system component is in control.

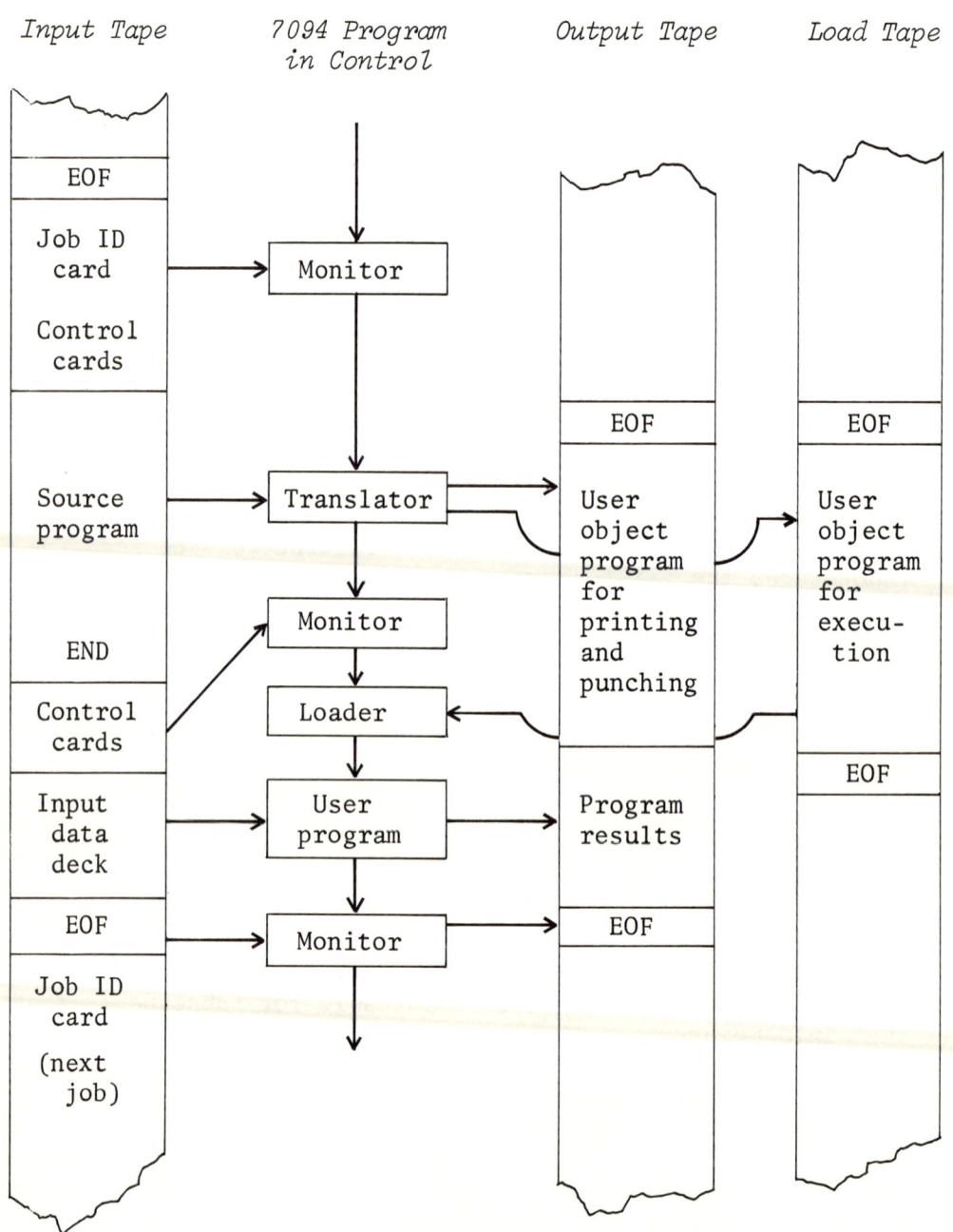

Figure 5.2

If the user job is a FORTRAN job, it may include more than one source program; the compiler will translate them one after another, stacking the object programs behind one another on the output and load tapes. When it has finished with the last, it transfers control back to the monitor. The input tape is now positioned after the END card of the last source program (there is only one source program illustrated in Figure 5.2). The monitor reads the input tape, scanning the control cards, and determines that the next block of cards is the execution-time data deck. Before the object program can be executed, the monitor must bring in another major system component, the *loader*, and give it control.

The function of the loader is to assemble, in main memory, the user's object program(s) and all required auxiliary subprograms. The object program, you remember, was written onto the load tape; if there were several programs translated, they have been stacked one behind the other, in object form, on the load tape. In another part of secondary storage are all the FORTRAN *library* programs, in binary form. The loader brings some of these into memory in response to explicit specifications by the user (as with the SQRT program, which is brought in if the program contains a statement referring to it). The loader brings in other library subprograms without explicit requests, in order to perform some functions that the user does not have to think about (for example, conversion of data from EBCDIC to floating-point format). All the necessary programs are brought into memory, and the loader sets up communication links between them. Because the setting up of these links is a major operation, the program that does it is sometimes called a *linkage editor*.

The loader now transfers control to the user's program. At this point (refer to Figure 5.2) the input tape is positioned in front of the input data. When the user's program reads the input tape (e.g., by a READ statement in a FORTRAN program), the first card-image will be read into memory. When the user's program writes on the output tape (e.g., by a WRITE statement), a record will be written for later off-line printing.

When the user's program is finished (e.g., by a STOP statement), control is automatically returned to the monitor. The monitor performs some final operations for this job, including making a record of the total amount of 7094 time it used (including monitor, translator, loader, and execution phases). The monitor also writes an end-of-file mark on the output tape, which is now ready for the output of the next job. Then the monitor reads the input tape, scanning the control cards of the next job, and the entire process is repeated.

3. *I/O Channels and Interrupts; a Chronicle of Wasted Time*

From the point of view of efficiency, the classic batch-processing system had two principal virtues: it prevented delays between jobs by batching them together, and it speeded up input/output by putting card-images and print-line-images on tape. Nevertheless, there were still problems arising from the discrepancies in speed between I/O and computation. To get an idea of the magnitude of the problem, we can consider a fairly specific analogy.

The Atalanta-Behemoth program can be paraphrased as follows: read a card, do some simple calculations, print a line, and repeat. Now imagine devoting a fairly advanced computer -- say, an IBM 360 Model 75 -- to this activity, giving it an on-line card reader and an on-line printer. Suppose we have a substantial amount of data -- 5,000 input data cards, for example -- so that we go through that loop many times. We can forget about the one-shot parts of the job, i.e., the time for the compiler, and some time spent on getting started and finishing up. If we just look at the time spent in executing that basic loop, we can estimate that for a 360/75 it would take roughly ten minutes to process 5,000 sets of Atalanta-Behemoth data. The really interesting thing about that ten minutes is that less than *one-third of a second* is required for the calculation; all the rest is I/O time.

This situation is analogous to one in which a research group hires a brilliant computational assistant at a brilliant salary, puts him in an office, and sets him to working out calculations on raw data by hand. It takes him an hour to do the calculations on one set of data. The data must be transmitted to him first, however, and his results must be transmitted too;

assuming that both data and results are transported by camel caravan between him and a remote desert oasis, it takes six weeks for him to get the data and six weeks for his results to be returned. This proportion of I/O time to computing time (roughly 2000 to 1) is the same as in the 360/75 case.

Now, if he operates in a manner similar to our 360/75 with on-line card reading and printing, what does he do? He sits quietly in his office for six weeks; a messenger arrives with a single set of data, whereupon he computes furiously for an hour; he hands the results to the messenger, who sets out on a round trip; the brilliant computational assistant sits quietly in his office for twelve weeks until the messenger appears with the next set of data.

To be more realistic, we should substitute tape drives for the on-line card reader and printer, with off-line card-to-tape and tape-to-printer operations, as it was done in the 7094 batch-processing system. This is analogous to using more modern forms of transportation to and from the Sahara. Pursuing the analogy, our computing friend will now sit, hands folded, for only eight days (round-trip time). Again, the proportions are the same as they would be with a 360/75 reading and writing tape.

Clearly this kind of situation would not be permitted in real life. What, in fact, would we do -- assuming that the minimum time to transmit data between the 'computer' and the Sahara could not be reduced beyond four days? Let us make another assumption: the only reason that a new set of data is not sent out until the results of the last set are received is that there is only one messenger. If that is the case, then one thing we might do is hire more messengers and send them out at one-day intervals. There would be four days to wait for the first, but after that one would arrive every day. The result of this scheme would be that our friend would be busy one hour each day, instead of one hour out of every eight days.

Another obvious efficiency would be to let each messenger carry more than one set of data; whether this is possible or not depends on the rate at which raw data are being collected in the desert. Under certain conditions, if the computational wizard is also a decent administrator, he might arrange to keep busy all the time by balancing the number of messengers, the amount of data each transports, and the various working and transportation speeds involved.

Finally -- and most obviously -- he can make use of any periods when he has to wait by having several projects going at once. He can compute away at some problem until the arrival of the messenger interrupts him; thereupon he marks his place in the other problem, files it carefully away, and attacks the news from the Sahara; an hour later he sends the messenger on his way, takes the other work out of the file, and picks up where he left off.

The analogy is beginning to creak and gape, as analogies will; nevertheless, the obvious steps toward improving the efficiency of the human computer are applicable to the electronic computer system as well. In summary, they are:

1. The transmission of input data for the next pass through a loop should be initiated before the current pass is completed.

2. More than one set of data should be transmitted at a time.

3. The computer should do some other useful work while it is waiting for input or output to be completed.

We should not sell the batch-processing system short; these ideas can to some degree be incorporated into a batch system. Their implementation depends on a device called an *I/O channel*. I/O channels are communication paths between the *main processor* (the central computer of a system) and the I/O devices attached to it. A channel is really a kind of small, special-purpose computer; it executes a limited range of operations, having to do with the manipulation of I/O devices. The most important thing about the channel concept is that the main processor can start up the channel and then go and do something else, without having to wait for the length of time it takes to transmit a record, for example, from magnetic tape to core storage (main memory).

If the main processor, executing a program, reaches the point where an input record is required, it requests input from the channel that lies between the CPU and the appropriate tape unit. The CPU is now free -- possibly idle -- while the channel activates the tape unit and transmits a record from tape to main memory, all without bothering the CPU. If the program is such that the CPU cannot do anything until the data are in, then the main processor is like the man who sits quietly in his office until the messenger arrives. Nevertheless, the fact that the CPU and the channel can be operating independently is going to prove useful.

Now, how does the CPU know when the data are in (or out, since the channel also takes care of transferring information from core storage to an I/O device)? There are basically two ways. The CPU can 'interrogate' the channel, by a special instruction that asks 'are you through yet?' The CPU can keep asking until the answer is yes, whereupon the new data can be processed. Alternatively, the channel can send a signal to the CPU announcing that it has finished the transmission. This signal, called an *asynchronous interrupt*,* causes an automatic transfer of control in the CPU from whatever it was doing to a section of programming that attends to the news from the channel. There is also a procedure whereby the CPU can 'mark its place' and return to what it was doing before the interruption occurred.

One way to make use of all this elegant apparatus is, roughly, to let the CPU ask the channel for data before the data are actually needed. Then, hopefully, when the CPU does need the data it will not have to wait so long. This is what the man in the office does when he asks for more messengers to start the trip before he has received the data from the first. While he is processing the first set of data, the second, third, fourth, and fifth messengers are on their way. The incoming data are stored by the channel into temporary storage areas in

---

* To those readers who care about the language, the author can only apologize for this grammatic barbarism. Computer technology moves forward at a fine, heady pace, and often drags language, kicking and screaming, behind it.

main memory; these areas are called *buffers*. When the program needs a fresh set of data, it gets it from a buffer.

Additional efficiency can be gained by a technique called *blocking*, which amounts to letting the messengers carry more than one set of data at a time. We have described a tape record as a block of related information, and implied that a single card is usually transcribed onto magnetic tape as a single record. Actually, what is important about a tape record is that it is the unit of information that is read or written by one I/O operation. It turns out that a long record is read in not much more time than a short one; this means that it is more efficient to read longer records. It is possible to transcribe a *block* of cards into a single tape record, and then read them all at once into a large buffer. If card images are stored on tape as individual records, they are said to be 'unblocked.' If fifty cards are transcribed as one record, they are said to be 'blocked,' with a blocking factor of fifty.

In the batch-processing system, both buffering and blocking can be used. It was suggested earlier that if the human calculator were also an able administrator, he might be able to keep himself busy by properly pacing the messengers and the amount of data they transported. Efficient use of a batch-processing system involves similar administrative care; some of this care has to be taken by the FORTRAN programmer, and some is automatically taken for him by the system. Nevertheless, for most problems, there is still a high percentage of time during which the CPU has no useful work.

What is missing is the most obvious solution that comes to mind in the human situation. If the main processor can work on several jobs at once, then we can make use of its idle time. The systems that are replacing batch-processing make use of this notion; they are generally called *multiprogramming systems*.

4. *Multiprogramming Systems*

Picture the memory of the computer as being divided into several partitions, each containing a program, as in Figure 5.3. Programs A, B, and C are completely independent user programs.

The control program -- which may go by the name of supervisor, monitor, or executive program -- is initally in control of the machine; that is, the CPU is getting instructions from the control partition.

The user programs have priorities. These priorities are either assigned by human administrative decisions (job A is more important than job B) or calculated by the system according to rules that improve the efficiency of the system. Let us assume, for the example of Figure 5.3, that program A has highest priority, program C has lowest. The control program gives control to program A first; the CPU begins executing instructions out of the A partition. The control program will get control back again on any of the following conditions:

(a) the program currently being executed asks for I/O (reaches a READ or WRITE statement);
(b) the program currently being executed reaches completion (reaches a STOP statement or attempts to do something illegal or impossible);
(c) a currently active channel signals completion by an asynchronous interrupt.

Initially, then, A is in control; eventually it will ask for I/O, and the supervisor will get control. The supervisor starts up a channel on behalf of program A, and notes that A has to wait until its request is satisfied. The supervisor notes where execution of A was suspended, and then gives control to the next program in its schedule of priorities -- program B. Now B keeps control until either it asks for I/O *or* the channel that is working for A signals completion of the I/O. The supervisor gets control and determines which of these conditions occurred. If B asked for I/O, it starts up another channel on B's behalf, saves information about the status of B, and gives control to program C. If, on the other hand, there was a channel interrupt for A, then the supervisor saves the status of B and returns control to A, which has higher priority; A has completed its I/O and can now continue.

When one of the programs reaches completion, the supervisor again gets control. It may then fetch a new user program that is waiting to be run, and put it into the now unused partition. The waiting user programs may be sitting in a card reader, or may have been 'queued' onto a high-speed device like a disk unit. These waiting job decks are the supervisor's input data. When the supervisor reads, it starts up a channel for itself and then finds useful work, from the job partitions, to fill the waiting time. Thus the use of an on-line card reader is not necessarily inefficient in this sort of system.

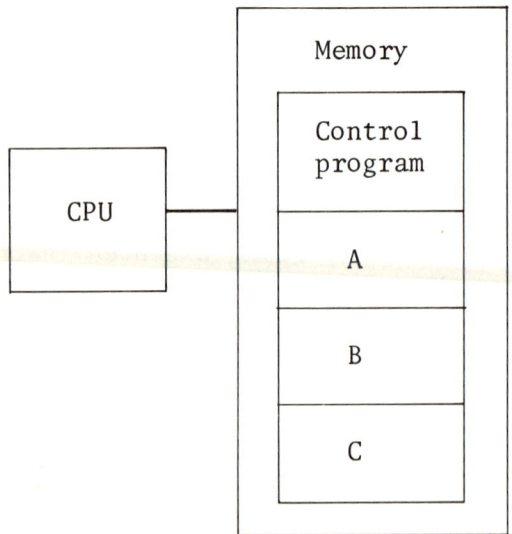

Figure 5.3

5. *System Evolution: Multiprocessor Systems*

The system just described is a kind of model of a multiprogramming system. Systems actually in use are likely to apply a variety of techniques in order to achieve what seems to be the maximum utilization of all available resources, and to optimize one or more possible conditions. There are various measures of the efficiency of computer systems. One is *throughput* -- the number of jobs or quantity of data that can be processed in a given period of time. Another is *turnaround time*: this is the interval from the time when the user first hands in his job to the time when he gets his results back. A system that maximizes throughput may reduce the efficiency of the users of the system by also maximizing turnaround time. On the other hand, a system that gives best service to its users by minimizing turn-around time may operate the computer at low efficiency. The ideal system, of course, maximizes throughput, minimizes turn-around time, and makes everybody happy.

Let's look at a real system, one that has been used at Columbia University. The name of the system is ASP (for Attached Support Processor). Figure 5.4 is a schematic diagram of the basic hardware configuration. It is called a *multiprocessor* system because it includes two computers, or processors. One is called the *main processor*, and is an IBM 360 Model 75; the other, called the *support processor*, is a 360 Model 50. (The IBM 360 is a line of computers with similar logic but varying in speed, capacity, and cost. The higher model numbers represent more speed, more storage capacity, and more money.)

The old 7094/1401 batch processing system had two computers, too, but it was not called a multiprocessor system. The difference lies in the fact that the two (or more) CPU's of a multiprocessor system are connected, by hardware, in such a way that they can communicate with each other, and can cooperate in various activities required for the processing of a job. (The ASP system is a rather atypical multiprocessor system, in that the two processors perform strictly separate functions, and operate, as we shall see, in a kind of master-slave relationship. In the more typical situation the processors are likely to be functionally equivalent. In fact, the purest definitions of multiprocessor systems describe a hardware configuration in which several CPU's share a common memory.)

ASP is an extension of OS/360, a standard operating system designed by IBM for the 360. OS/360 comes in a variety of forms and can be to some extent tailored to the needs of a particular installation. The ASP/OS system allows considerable flexibility with respect to the kinds and distribution of I/O devices -- called 'peripheral hardware' -- and some flexibility with respect to the CPU's employed. There are still other

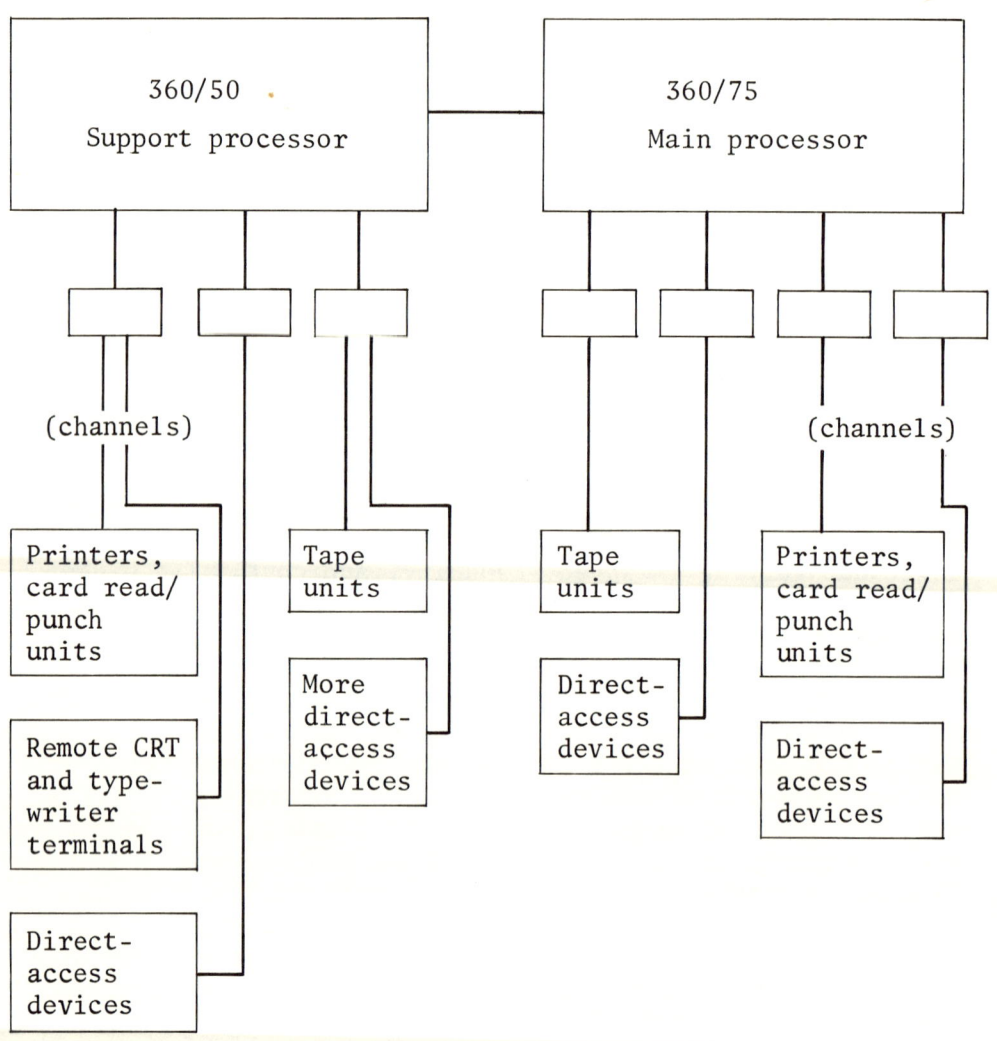

Figure 5.4

systems that implement the basic ideas of the ASP system in different ways.

In the system delineated in Figure 5.4, the support processor is occupied by a multiprogrammed supervisory system. Instead of running a number of concurrent user programs, it executes a number of concurrent 'system' programs that provide support functions for user programs. The best way to see what these support functions consist of is to see what happens to user programs running under ASP.

Assume that the user program is on cards: control cards, FORTRAN source deck, input data deck. These cards are stacked in a card reader attached to the support processor. One of the programs in the support processor, while it has control, reads in the deck and copies it (writing blocked card-images) onto a direct-access device (a disk, for example). This program also examines some of the control cards, which may determine the priority of the job. The job, with its associated priority, now resides on the disk with other waiting jobs, in what is called the *job queue*.

The main processor is under control of a standard operating system, which resembles the 7094 batch-processing system in that it executes one job at a time, finishing one completely before it goes on to the next. Again, the job may require that the main processor system invoke one or more translators and a loader before giving control to the user object program.

The big difference, however, is that instead of reading jobs from a card reader or an input tape, the main processor system 'reads' them from the support processor. The two processors are linked, by hardware, in such a way that each looks like an I/O device to the other. When the system in the main processor needs a new job, the support processor picks the job with highest priority in the job queue, reads it from the disk, and transmits it to the main processor. This memory-to-memory transmission is very fast. The support processor provides buffering by reading the next job into its own memory before the main processor actually asks for it.

When the job running in the main processor generates output

for printing or punching, the output information is sent over to the support processor. The support processor ships it out to another disk unit, into an *output queue*. Another support program selects jobs from this queue and routes them to printers and punch units attached to the support processor.

An important function of the support processor is keeping track of the running time of jobs on the main processor. Associated with each job is its expected running time, which is specified by the programmer. If a job runs longer than its time estimate, the operating system should shut it off, particularly because excessive running time is most likely a symptom of errors in the program. The support processor, in ASP, is used to monitor jobs in the main processor, and to remove from the main processor any jobs that run overtime.*

At a given time, when this system is in full swing, there will be many jobs in various stages of processing. If there are several card readers, a new job may be being read in each (by one or more 'reader' support programs). Several jobs will be waiting in the job queue on the disk. One job will be 'next to be run,' and a support program will be moving it from the queue into a buffer in support-processor main memory. One job will be in execution on the main processor. Several jobs will be in the output queue, waiting to be printed and punched. If there are several printers, each will be printing a job, under control of a corresponding number of 'print' support programs; the same will hold true for card-punch units.

Since the support processor is multiprogrammed, these active support programs are all in memory at once. Most of them are doing I/O most of the time, so each requires relatively little CPU time. The system requires delicate adjustment -- for example, of the priorities of the support programs -- in order to achieve an effective balance of all these simultaneous functions. When it is well tuned, however, it provides

---

* It was stated earlier that the two ASP processors have a kind of master-slave relationship. The reader is invited to consider the following philosophical question: which is the master?

significantly more throughput and shorter turn-around times than could be achieved by running the two processors independently, each with a standard system.

Actually there may be time to spare in the support processor. If so, additional support functions can be added. In particular, remote terminals (typewriters and cathode-ray-tube devices) can be handled by an ASP system. From these terminals, users can enter jobs into the queue for execution on the main processor; for example, one of the support functions can examine FORTRAN statements as they come in from a terminal, immediately inform the user of mistakes (misspelling of key words, illegal syntax, etc.), and allow him to correct the statement right away.

One consequence of providing many support functions is that although there may be enough CPU time to perform them all, there may not be enough main memory space to hold all the programs. In the discussion of the 7094 batch-processing system it was pointed out that a monitor, several translators, and a loader could not all fit into main memory at once. When one of these programs gave way to another, the new one was loaded into memory on top of the preceding one, thereby erasing the preceding one. Fresh copies of all these routines were kept on the system tape, so they could always be loaded in again.

A similar situation holds in the main-processor system in ASP. The supervisory program interprets control cards, determines that the FORTRAN compiler, for example, must be loaded, and brings the compiler into main memory from secondary storage. If the compilation step is to be followed by loading and execution of the user program, the loader (or linkage editor) is brought in to overlay the compiler; the user program in turn will overlay the loader. In essence, the reason for overlaying is that the total number of instructions in the compiler, the loader, and the user program is likely to exceed the total capacity of main memory.

In many cases an individual program is too large to fit in core memory; this is true of many versions of the FORTRAN compiler. Such a program can be broken up into relatively independent sections; when one section is finished, it can cause itself to be overlaid by the next section, brought in from secondary storage. This process is sometimes called *dynamic loading*: programs, or sections thereof, are loaded when they are needed, as opposed to the situation where everything that will be required is loaded from the start.

In the support processor, dynamic loading is the normal mode of operation. In the system depicted in Figure 5.4, the total memory space required for all the support programs plus the ASP supervisor is roughly twice the size of the 360/50 memory. When a support program has completed its current function, it may be overlaid by another support program, required for a new task, which is brought in from secondary storage. One of the disk units, for example, may serve as the permanent residence of all the 'dynamic' support programs.

The ASP system, then, combines several system techniques -- multiple processors, multiprogramming, dynamic loading, and standard sequential job-processing -- to achieve effective operation in a rather sophisticated way. There are a number of changes that can be made to ASP, however, which may be regarded as stages in the evolution of an operating system. Let us run through some of these rather briefly.

First, if multiprogramming is as effective as it would seem to be, then it makes sense to use it on the main processor. The programs in execution on the main processor are doing a lot of I/O: job decks and print/punch output are handled via the support processor, which is a special kind of I/O unit, while tape and direct/access I/O, including loading of programs, is done through channels attached to the main processor. Time may be wasted during I/O operations unless the main processor operates with a partitioned multiprogramming system like the one described in Section 4. We could thus have a system like the one represented in Figure 5.5. The two processors play the same roles as before, but the main processor system now looks like the system of Figure 5.3.

It is worth noting here that the partitions labeled 'job partition' may be occupied by user jobs or by miniature systems -- called 'subsystems' -- that create an environment within which a special set of user jobs operate. One such subsystem might be more or less permanently resident in a partition. It should also be observed that the number and size of the partitions need not be fixed, but may vary to conform to the memory requirements of the jobs being executed.

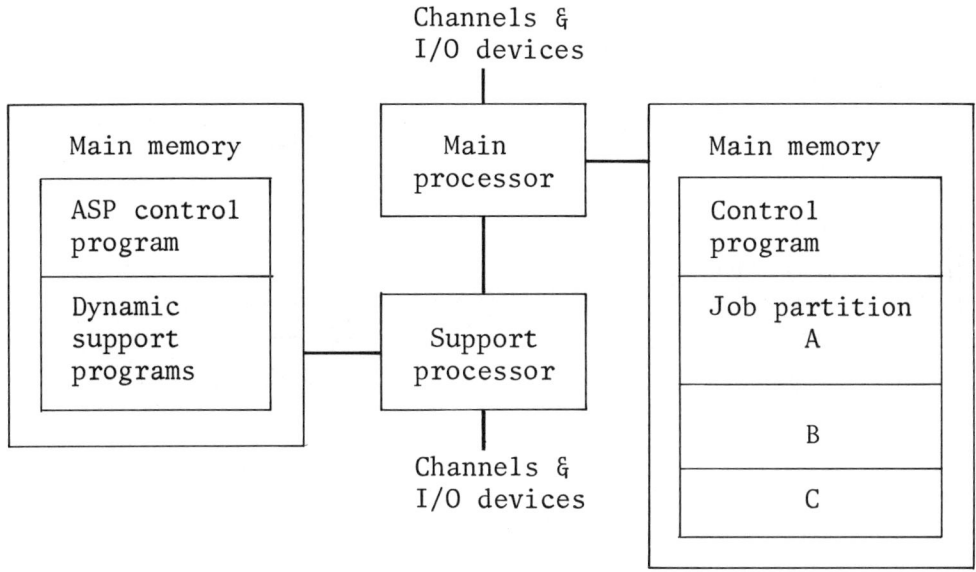

Figure 5.5

If the support processor is big and fast enough, the ASP functions may still not use all its power, or need all its core memory. ASP itself, then, may operate out of a single partition of the support processor, while there are other multiprogramming partitions devoted to user jobs. Now we have really lost the distinction between support processor and main processor. We have, rather, a 'support partition.' The other partitions are to it what the main processor was to the support processor.

As a result of this idea, we can dispense with the support processor altogether. In Figure 5.6, everything has gone back into one machine. This assumes, of course, that the computer being used has enough resources -- memory space, CPU speed, and peripheral I/O devices or secondary storage -- to handle the work formerly done by two machines.

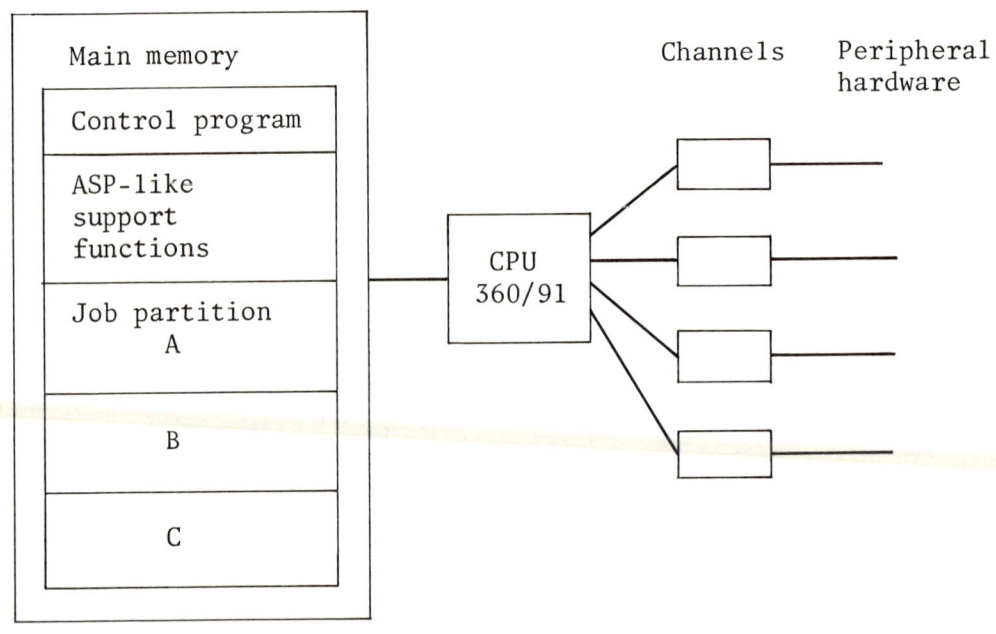

Figure 5.6

Finally, Figure 5.7 illustrates a similar system implemented at Columbia University. There are two machines, but no logical change has been made over the system of Figure 5.6. The second computer (the Model 75) has been added in order to extend the power of the system. It functions as an extension of the Model 91, increasing the total resources of the system -- again, memory, CPU time, and secondary storage. Whether one implements this system or the single-processor version depends simply on how much computing power one can use.

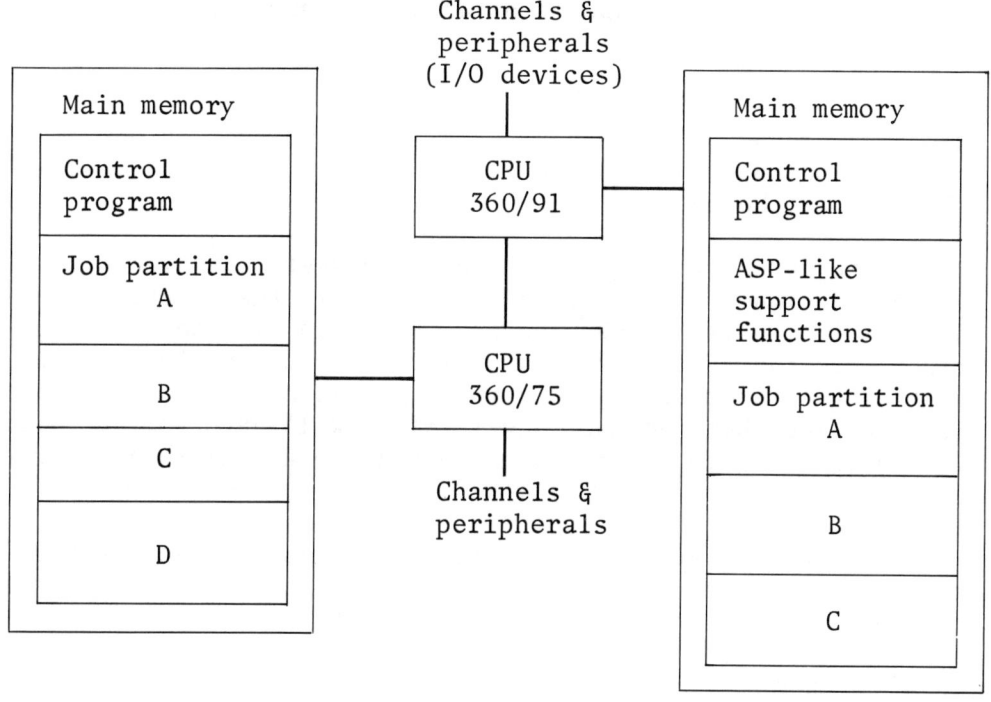

Figure 5.7

6. *Time-Slicing*

The multiprogramming system described in Section 4 has the virtue of filling in the gaps in the CPU's productive time by letting it work on another program when the current one is waiting for I/O. This will increase the total *throughput* of the system. Now let us direct our attention to reducing the *turn-around* time for most of the users of the system.

In the 7094 batch-processing system, a user must wait until:

>a full batch of jobs is collected;
>
>they are put on an input tape;
>
>the entire batch is run on the 7094;

> the output tape is printed and punched;
>
> the paper and punched cards are sorted out and his own are returned to him.

His turn-around time, then, is not just dependent on how long his own job runs, but on the length of all the stages of all the jobs in the batch.

With the multiprogrammed super-ASP system described at the end of Section 5, there are several factors that improve turn-around time. First, when the user hands in his job it can go right into the card reader, and from there to the input queue. There may be a queue at the card reader as well as on the input-queue device, but the user who is first will have some priority. In the 7094 system, there was no advantage at all in being first on the input tape.

Second, the system can contain mechanisms for computing appropriate priorities for jobs. One mechanism that is fairly popular is this: each user includes in his control cards a maximum time for his job. The system will give higher priority to a job that will run less than a minute, and low priority to one that expects to run for six hours. Thus if you, with your one-minute job, come in right after a six-hour grinder, you will probably be run first. It seems fair, and helpful, not to make a short job wait for a long one.

At this point it may be helpful to divide programs into two classes, and to introduce two new terms to describe them. If we consider how a program would behave if it had the whole machine (no multiprogramming), we will see that many programs spend much more time on I/O than on computing. That is to say, even with buffering, blocking, and reasonable attempts in the program to prevent excessive CPU idle time by overlapping computing and channel activity, this type of program spends a major amount of time waiting for the I/O to catch up. Such programs are called *I/O-bound*. Alternatively, some jobs do great amounts of computing, and what little I/O they do can take place with no idle CPU time at all. Programs like this are called *computation-bound*, by contrast. (Of course, using the machine more for computation than for I/O isn't a *bind*; it's using the machine efficiently.)

In some cases, however, computation-bound jobs can be troublesome. A long, computation-bound job may be given low priority in a multiprogramming system; eventually, though, it must be run, and in some cases it may have high priority at some point. Now, a top-priority job being executed in a multiprogramming system will give up control of the machine (compare Section 4) when it asks for I/O. Thus a job that computes for a long time without doing any I/O may monopolize the CPU for significant periods of time. This is not bad for the overall efficiency of the system, but it may penalize the lower-priority user, who doesn't get a chance at his few seconds' worth of CPU for a long time.

There is a technique called *time-slicing* that seeks to remedy this situation. It requires a hardware and a software modification to our stylized multiprogramming system. The hardware change is the addition of a kind of clock called an *interval timer*. This is something like a kitchen timer (but it is internal to the computer); it can be set to 'go off' -- that is, to cause an interrupt -- at the end of a desired interval of time.

Now the supervisory program will get control on any of the following conditions:

    (a)   the program currently being executed asks for I/O;

    (b)   the program reaches completion;

    (c)   a channel signals completion with an interrupt;

or   (d)   the clock goes off.

Looking at it the other way around, when a user program gets control of the CPU, it will have to *relinquish* that control on any of the following conditions:

    (a)   the program needs I/O;

    (b)   the program has reached completion;

    (c)   a program *with higher priority* is ready to run because its I/O request is satisfied;

(d) the program has run more than its allotted time and has not lost control because of conditions 1, 2, or 3.

The supervisor assigns a time-slice to each job. Just before a job gets control, the supervisor sets the interval timer to go off when the allotted time is up. Thus a computation-bound job cannot monopolize the CPU. It should be obvious that the length of a time-slice is a crucial variable in such a system, and the optimal value is not easily determined. It will surely change from installation to installation, and in a given installation it may change from day to day or from hour to hour. The time-slice may be determined 'dynamically' by the system itself; that is, it may constantly be changed on the basis of what is happening in the system at any point in time.

7. *Time-Sharing or Interactive Systems*

The last type of computer system that we are going to consider is one that has traditionally been known as a *time-sharing* system. The term 'time-sharing' has come to be criticized as misleading or meaningless; it does, however, have the support of history. As we shall see shortly, it may be more fitting to distinguish systems of this type as *interactive* systems. Before discussing the purposes and organization of such systems, we should develop a few preliminary concepts and terms.

First of all, let us define an *active* program (or an active job) as one that is either (a) currently being executed by the main-processor CPU, or (b) temporarily suspended in mid-execution because it has requested I/O or has been interrupted. Jobs in the input queue are *inactive,* as are jobs that have completed the execution phase but are in an output queue waiting to be printed. In the multiprogramming systems described earlier, whether or not time-slicing is used, all simultaneously active jobs are in memory at once. The amount of memory any job can use is limited by the size of available memory space, the number of jobs that are active at the same time, and the memory requirements of each of them. Looking at it the other way around, the number of jobs that may be concurrently active depends on the memory requirements of the jobs and the total memory capacity of the machine.

Second, we define something called the *state* of an active program, in the following way. When a program is first loaded into memory, it consists of a set of computer instructions, a set of initial data items, and a set of reserved areas for information that will be developed during program execution. These elements reside in an area of memory -- the 'program area' -- which is of course composed of a set of memory registers. The *initial state* of the program is defined by the contents of all the memory registers in the program area.

Once the program begins to be executed, its state changes in two important ways. First, it begins to use CPU registers, in addition to memory registers. The CPU registers are used for arithmetic (and other) operations on data, and at any point in time may contain partial results of such operations that have not yet been stored in memory. The CPU also contains a register that indicates which instruction is next to be executed. The state of these registers during execution thus becomes part of the state of the program. If the program is interrupted, the state of the CPU registers must be preserved if execution of the program is to be resumed later on.

The other change in a program during execution is in the state of its memory area. The most obvious change of this type takes place in the data area as computations are performed and new information is generated. A look back at Exercise 3.1 will make this clear. Instruction sequences may also be modified, although this is less common, especially in computers like the 360. Finally, the extent of the program area may change; it is sometimes desirable for a program to 'grow' or 'shrink' as its memory requirements change during execution.

Now, in all the systems we have seen so far, a program can be interrupted, and continued later, provided that it remains in memory after the interruption. It is also necessary to preserve the state of the CPU registers at the time of the interruption, since they will be used, and their contents altered, by the next program to be executed. The contents of these registers can be saved in an area of memory reserved for such information, and associated with the particular program to which they belong.

One of the distinctive features of a time-sharing system is that many jobs may be active at once -- more than can fit into memory at once. When a program is interrupted, it may, if necessary, be temporarily removed from memory. This is accomplished by writing out, onto a high-speed secondary storage device (a disk or drum, for example), a copy of the entire state of the program when it was interrupted. This simply means writing out the contents of the program area plus the contents of the CPU registers. This information is written in such a way that when it is later read back, everything can be restored to its former state and execution of the program can be resumed. The process of writing the state of a program onto secondary storage is sometimes called 'rolling out,' while restoring the program state is called 'rolling in.'

Basically, then, a time-sharing system is like a multiprogramming system with time-slicing, and with this additional feature: the number of active programs is not confined to the number that can fit into memory, because active programs can be 'rolled out' to secondary storage. It follows from this fact that the potential size of a job is not necessarily limited by the size of other jobs that are active at the same time. In a time-sharing system, when the current job is interrupted (for example, because its time-slice is up) it may turn out that the next job to be run is not in memory. The job just interrupted may be rolled out to make room for the new one. If the new one is large, several jobs may have to be rolled out. During the process of rolling-out and rolling-in, which is entirely a matter of input and output, the CPU can be devoted to some work that is not involved in this 'swapping' of programs.

There is no clear gain in efficiency here; in fact, time-sharing is generally less efficient than a well-tuned multiprogramming system. The justification for all this sophistication lies in the fact that time-sharing techniques permit what is probably the ultimate in convenience for the user. In order to see this, we need to stop looking at the inside of the system and turn to its external aspect: how does it look to the user?

Imagine that you are sitting in your office, and you have diagrammed, on paper, the computer solution to a problem. In a corner of your office is a typewriter terminal connected by telephone lines to the computer. You sit down at the terminal, pick up the phone, and dial the computer. It responds with some message indicating that your slightest wish is its command, and after entering some control information, you begin to write a FORTRAN program on the typewriter.

Naturally, you make mistakes. If you type a statement incorrectly, the computer will respond with a message indicating that, in its role as a FORTRAN language machine, it cannot understand you. You then correct the statement and go on. The machine may be able to correct some errors by making some assumptions about what you meant; it will inform you of such assumptions. When you have completed the program, you ask that it be compiled. If the compiler encounters any difficulties, it will tell you so immediately; again, you will be able to make corrections.

You can test the program, as soon as it has been compiled, by typing input data at the terminal. If the answers are wrong, you can correct the program and try again. Not only are you getting essentially instant turn-around, but you are carrying on a conversation with the machine. This conversational ability is what makes the term 'interactive' a good one to describe this sort of system. The point is that you do not have to set everything up in advance -- complete program plus input data -- hand it over to the computer operators, and go away for several hours, hoping for the best. You can make adjustments and corrections as you go along.

What follows, by way of illustration, is an annotated scenario of a session at a time-sharing terminal. Whatever is printed in italics is typed by the computer, the rest is typed by the user. The small numerals on the left refer to the notes that follow.

The user begins by saying he wants to create a FORTRAN program called 'abdc.' The computer tells him he has to identify himself first. When the computer is asking for information, it types out a question mark; this signal appears at the beginning of many of the lines that follow.

```
             create Fortran program abdc
         sign in, please.
         ? I am Tristram Shandy, user code 68-298, account no. B-15
         okay.  you have 15.27 minutes of CPU time left in your account.
         ? create Fortran program abdc
1        100       raed c, t
         unrecognizable statement.
2        100       read c, t
         200       d = sqrt ((4920 * t/2) ** 2 - (c/2) ** 2
         missing 1 right parenthesis(es).  I put it (them) at the end:
         200       d = sqrt ((4920 * t/2) ** 2 - (c/2) ** 2)
3        300       print d
         400       go to 2
4        500 !compile
         trouble with statement 400: go to 2
         statement 2 not found.
5        ? 400:2:100
         400       go to 100
         ? compile
         compilation successful.
         ? execute
6             c=? 5000.
              t=? 5.0
              d=  12289.8320
              c=? 5000.
              t=? 1.0
              d=  12043.2539
7             c=? quit,
         ? sign off
         you used 0.18 minutes and you have 15.09 minutes left.
```

Notes:

1. While the user is creating a program, the system automatically types a number at the beginning of each line. This number serves to identify the line for future reference. The numbers go up by 100 each time, so that the user can easily insert statements in between or wherever he wishes.

2. The system rejected the statement, so it issues the old line number again.

3. After the computer types '300', the user can, if he wishes, reject the machine's interpretation of statement 200. If he wants to accept it, he simply types in the next statement.

4. The user doesn't want any statement 500; he types '!' indicating that he's giving an order, not entering a FORTRAN statement. The order is that the program be compiled.

5. This means: "in statement 400, change '2' to '100'." The computer displays the corrected statement.

6. During execution, 'read' statements are normally interpreted as requests for input from the terminal. The system cues the user with the name of each variable listed in the 'read' statement; the user then enters a value. On output, the system gives the variable name before typing out the value.

7. There is a special button on the terminal, marked 'quit' (or 'interrupt,' or 'cancel,' or something similar). When the user hits this button, the system stops whatever it is doing for him, which in this case was waiting for input from the terminal. It types 'quit,' to acknowledge the interruption, then types a question mark and waits for fresh orders. In this example, the quit button is used to get out of the program, which, you may have observed, is written in the form of an endless loop. The quit button is handy for this purpose, and for others as well.

Two days later, the user comes back to the terminal and the following dialogue takes place:

I am Tristram Shandy, user code 68-298, account no. B-15.
okay. you have 15.09 minutes of CPU time left in your account.
? execute program abdc
      c=? 2000.
      t=? 1.28
      d= *2985.7886*
      c=? quit,

and so forth.

The program that was created in the earlier session has

been saved, and can be executed any time. It can also be
changed and recompiled; the user can add, change, or delete
statements. If he wants to scrap the whole thing, he can ask
that program 'abdc' be made to disappear.

   The advantages to the user, in this system, may be summa-
rized thus:

   (a) the full capabilities of a large-scale computer system
        are available from a remote, conveniently located
        terminal;
   (b) programs and files of data are kept for him by the
        system, and he can gain access to them merely by
        naming them at the terminal;
   (c) he can work at his own pace at the terminal, but is
        charged only for CPU time that he actually uses;
   (d) the amount of time that elapses between his typing a
        request and receiving a response from the system is
        short in terms of human response times.

   These advantages can be had because the system makes use
of the time-sharing concept. The user is only one of perhaps
a hundred people simultaneously working at remote terminals.
The maximum number of simultaneous users that a system will
support depends ultimately on the power of the central computer, but the basic principle is that the computer is faster
than any one person really needs.

   The trouble with the other systems we have described --
even the most sophisticated -- is that the individual user does
not really profit from the speed of the computer. A high-speed
computer may be able to carry out your computation in two
seconds; but you may have to wait in several queues for a few
hours before you get the answers that it took two seconds to
find. It is probably the case that you want results in a few
minutes; you neither need results in two seconds nor want to
wait several hours.

   This is particularly true when you are constructing and
testing a new program, as in the example above. There the
programmer made three errors. In a noninteractive system at
least two separate job-submittals would have been required --

one to find the errors, and another to run the corrected program. If turn-around time in the system were two hours, the programmer would have at least four hours of 'idle time' on his hands. If turn-around time were twenty-four hours -- not unusual in batch systems -- his attention to the problem would be seriously fragmented. In the interactive system, he spends about fifteen minutes of concentrated activity on the whole process. One can regard the time-sharing system as a matter of intensifying the degree of multiprogramming in the computer in order to decrease the necessity for multiprogramming the programmer (i.e., filling his idle time).

The system works roughly as follows: there are a large number (say one thousand) of remote terminals linked to the system. In order to use a terminal, a user 'dials in' and 'signs on.' Probabilities being what they are, at any given time some fraction -- say a tenth -- of the terminals will be signed on to the system. The users at these terminals represent *potential* jobs in the time-sliced, interactive, multiprogramming system.

Notice, however, that in the terminal session outlined above the user, who was signed on for about fifteen minutes, used only 0.18 minute of CPU time. That is, the actual demand he made on the CPU amounted to roughly one percent of the total period during which he was signed on. The other ninety-nine percent of the time he was: typing (slowly, by computer standards); waiting for responses to be typed back (quickly by his standards, but slowly by the machine's); thinking; scratching his head; and probably letting his mind wander occasionally.

Well, if by working at his own comfortable, natural pace, the programmer uses the computer at about one percent efficiency, then it makes sense to suppose that a hundred people could share it simultaneously on the same terms.* By 'overlapping'

---

* The figures quoted here should not be taken as in any sense standard or precise; they are reasonable for purposes of illustration. Interactive systems are still in the developmental stage, and none can be regarded as typical. Performance statistics vary widely with the nature of the specific hardware and software characteristics of the system.

computation for one user with terminal I/O and other I/O time
(including rolling jobs in and out of memory), and by applying
the time-slicing technique to those users that are actually
competing for the CPU at the same time, we can slow the computer down, so to speak, to the individual user's natural pace.

Because of the 'roll-out--roll-in' technique, jobs initiated from terminals can be accommodated in the system even if
there are already more active jobs than can fit in memory at
once. This makes it possible for time-slicing to be applied to
all these active programs. Because of the time-slicing technique, each active user can be given a fair share of the CPU's
attention, and can thus get fast responses from the system.

For any such system there is going to be a limit to the
number of users that can be signed on at the same time. Beyond
that limit, the system will slow down too much; it will become
sluggish, and the users will begin to feel restless waiting
for responses. Until that limit is reached, however, the users
are getting what from their point of view is immediate turn-
around. Experiments with interactive systems suggest that
programmers do function more efficiently with this type of
facility. The net amount of programmer time spent on the solution of a given problem tends to be smaller with an interactive than a non-interactive system; in some cases, the net
amount of computer time may be smaller, too.

A few concluding remarks about interactive systems are in
order. First, it is important that the system be able to keep
programs and data files, for each potential user, in some form
of secondary storage. This means that the hardware configuration must include a large amount of on-line, high-speed, large-
capacity secondary storage. It also means that the software
must include programs that do a lot of bookkeeping for the user
in an efficient and flexible manner.

The software must also include programs that have counterparts in the non-interactive systems -- compilers, for example
-- but that have been redesigned for the interactive environment. In particular, these programs must be conversational,
designed on the assumption that the user is present at the terminal while the program is being executed. When appropriate,

the program should engage the user in immediate decision-making, resolution of ambiguities, and modification of the program. Interactive systems tend to give rise to a whole new style in programming.

This style is useful for certain types of computer applications. In other cases, however, programs are more successfully implemented in the 'closed' or non-interactive style. Large-scale, long-running, 'production' programs that do massive computations or operate on massive amounts of data may be inappropriate for interactive operation. In particular, if the problem is always clearly defined, there is nothing gained by allowing the user to monitor the results during execution. Many scientific calculations are of this type. (As a counter-example, consider a program designed to search a machine-stored bibliography and print out titles relevant to a particular subject. Defining the criteria for selection may not be easy. The program might make trial choices and ask the user to confirm whether it is on the right track. A poor statement of the criteria might give rise to a thousand titles; the user at a terminal could stop this excessive response by using the 'quit' button.)

There are several ways for an installation that uses time-sharing to accommodate those programs that do not benefit from interaction. For one, the interactive system can be run only during certain hours; when it is not running, a different software system can be run to process the large, closed, production programs. Time-sharing might be run during the day, for example, and a batch system run overnight.

Alternatively, if the computer itself is powerful enough, there may not be enough work from the time-sharing users to absorb all of its time. A closed production program can be introduced into the system as a low-priority 'background' job; it will be run whenever the CPU has nothing else to do. During 'prime time' for interactive jobs (which will have higher priority), the background job will be interrupted frequently, and probably little of it will be executed. During the small hours of the night, however, the background jobs will probably sail through.

As we pointed out earlier, most of the development of operating systems has been motivated by the desire to use an expensive piece of equipment as efficiently as possible. Interactive systems, on the other hand, tend to put a higher premium on the convenience of the user (and consequently on his own efficiency.) As one might anticipate, systems of this type are more expensive. The computer is used less efficiently, partly because of the time devoted to rolling jobs in and out of memory, and the requirement for keeping track of the users' programs and data files in on-line storage. As of this writing, although it is universally accepted that interactive systems are a good idea, they are by no means universally accepted as standard operating systems. The next few years, however, will probably find interactive techniques developed to the point where they are acceptable on economic grounds.

CHAPTER 6

FURTHER STEPS IN COMPUTER PROBLEM-SOLVING

Chapter 2 outlined five steps leading up to the *Atalanta-Behemoth* program: problem definition, analysis, computational procedure, flow diagram, and coding. In general, these phases are described in terms of three, rather than five steps: problem definition, development of an algorithm, and implementation. An *algorithm* is a precisely specified method for providing a solution to a problem. An algorithm is not a program, because it is not written explicitly for a particular computing device. Implicitly, however, it must take into account the capabilities of the kind of device that is to be used. *Implementation* of an algorithm, which embraces the flow diagramming and coding steps described earlier, consists of redefining the algorithm as an ordered series of steps, each of which is a basic operation that the computing device 'knows' how to perform. Instances of such basic operations are: an internal hardware operation; a FORTRAN statement; or a subprogram like SQRT.

We must now consider four further steps that follow the writing of a program: testing, debugging, documentation, and production. *Testing* consists of submitting the program with a small amount of selected input data. The data should be selected in order to provide verification of the test results; they should be values for which we know the results in advance, and which test various possible contingencies in the program.

Debugging is the name for finding and correcting the causes of erroneous results. In order to be able to correct a program, the user needs some familiarity with the kind of output to be expected from a computer run. The remaining sections of this chapter will be devoted to a discussion of expected and unexpected computer output.

Once a program is fully debugged, it can be applied to processing the real input data for which it was designed. This is known as putting it into *production*. First, however, a careful record should be made of how the program works. Specifically, this *documentation* should include: what methods were used to

solve the problem; what form the input data should take; what
output should be expected; and any special requirements for
running the program, including whatever assumptions the programmer has made about the hardware and software environment.

In order to illustrate the nature -- and the difficulties
-- of debugging a program in an operating system, this chapter
is devoted to an examination of the results of actual encounters
with a specific operating system. The programs used for illustration are the two that were developed in earlier chapters.
If the reader has been able to run these jobs on a computer, he
should find it illuminating to compare his results with those
illustrated here. They are almost certain to be different,
but similar; there are useful conclusions to be drawn from both
the similarities and the differences.

For readers who are unable to gain access to a suitable
computer system, what follows is a reasonable substitute.

The operating system in which these jobs were run was the
ASP/OS/360 system described in Chapter 5, Section 5. At the
heart of this system were an IBM 360/50 as support processor,
and an IBM 360/75 as main processor. The hardware configuration was as illustrated in Figure 5.4. The operating system was
much as described there.

1. *Punched Output*

The items that are returned to the user after his jobs have
been run are:

    (a) the input deck for each job;
    (b) another deck of cards (only for job ABDC) which is the compiled object deck;
    (c) a sheaf of continuous-form paper, generally called an output *listing*, for each job.

The input deck is returned in its original state, and may
be used again. If the program must be modified, the user can
simply replace those cards that need changing and resubmit the
input deck.

The object deck contains the executable machine-code instructions generated by the compiler, along with other information required for execution of the program. This includes: constants used in the program, appropriately converted to binary form; the names of subprograms implicitly or explicitly referred to by the main program; requirements for memory space reserved for data areas. This deck, with some changes in the control cards, could be substituted for the source program in the job deck. The compilation step would then be omitted. In other words, if the program is satisfactory, it is unnecessary to translate it again. Programs used in the production phase are usually submitted in object-deck form.

If a program is going to be run only once or twice, however, there is little point in creating an object deck. Furthermore, programs of significant length or complexity usually have 'bugs' the first time they are run, and several trials are necessary to get the bugs out. During the debugging phase an object deck is of little use. Consequently the generation of an object deck is not usually automatic. In the Columbia system, the user must specifically request it or he will not get one. Later on we shall see how the request was made for the ABDC job, and that it was omitted in the deck for GEOM.

Even if a deck is requested, it will not be generated in the presence of a certain class of program errors. The errors may make it impossible for the compiler to generate a deck, or there may be mechanisms in the system that block the creation of a deck if severe errors exist in the source program. In such cases the deck will be missing, and information describing the cause of the failure will be found in the printed output.

Some user programs generate punched output. (In FORTRAN, a PUNCH statement is analogous to the PRINT statement, but produces punched cards.) It may be convenient to put results on punched cards if the results are to serve as input to another program *and* if the volume of output is small. If the volume is such that the output deck is more than a few inches thick, this procedure is inadvisable. Magnetic tape and direct-access devices are preferable data-storage media.

2. *The Printed Listing*

Figure 6.1 is the printed results of running job ABDC under the conditions described earlier. A minor amount of editing has been done in the interests of readability. In some cases several pages of the listing have been superimposed; the page numbers in the figure correspond to the original listing pages. Let's take it a page at a time.

Page 1 contains messages written by the ASP system running in the support processor (we'll call that ASP, for brevity's sake). The input deck is first read by ASP; whenever ASP encounters a control card, it prints it out as a kind of log of the major parts of the job. All the control cards of ABDC have been written out on page 1, the job deck has been completely read and put away in the input queue. The concluding remarks on this page may be ignored for the purposes of this discussion.

Page 2 contains messages written by the main processor, once it has received the job from the input queue and is ready to run it. First it reads and prints the JOB card. Next it reads the EXEC card. To say EXECute FORTHCLG is an abbreviated way of saying the following:

"This job is to consist of three job *steps*. The first step is called 'FORT', and the program to be executed in this step is the FORTRAN compiler. The input for this step is here in the deck, preceded by a control card of the form

    //FORT.SYSIN DD *

and followed by a '/*' card.

"The next step is called 'LKED', and the program to be executed is the *linkage editor* (which roughly corresponds to the 'loader' discussed earlier). The input to this step is the compiled program generated by the first step. The third step is called 'GO', and the program to be executed is the one set up for execution by the second step. The input to this step is here in the deck, preceded by a card of the form

    //GO.SYSIN DD *

and followed by a '/*' card."

```
                                                                    Page 1


//JDHABDC  JOB (████████),J.HELLWIG
//   EXEC  FORTHCLG,PARM.FORT='LIST,DECK',PARM.LKED='MAP'
//FORT.SYSIN DD *
/*
//GO.SYSIN DD *
/*
R=IHC002I STOP        0
R=IEC202I K 171,
R=IEF161I READER CLOSED
```

```
                                                                    Page 2

//JDHABDC  JOB (████████),J.HELLWIG
IEF236I ALLOC. FOR JDHABDC   FORT
IEF237I SYSPUNCH ON 173
IEF237I SYSUT1    ON 1C0
IEF237I SYSLIN    ON 1C0
IEF237I SYSUT2    ON 1C0
IEF237I SYSIN     ON 171
```

```
                                                                    Page 3

LEVEL 15 ( 1 JAN 68)                             OS/360    FORTRAN H

        COMPILER OPTIONS - NAME=  MAIN,OPT=02,LINECNT=50,SOURCE,EBCDIC,LIST,
                                  DECK,LOAD,NOMAP,NOEDIT,NOID,NOXREF


   ISN 0002      1        PRINT 7
   ISN 0003      2        READ 8, C, T
   ISN 0004      3        IF (C .EQ. 0) STOP
   ISN 0006      4        D = SQRT ((4920 * T/2)**2 - (C/2)**2)
   ISN 0007      5        PRINT 9, C, T, D
   ISN 0008      6        GO TO 2
   ISN 0009      7        FORMAT ('1       ATALANTA - BEHEMOTH DEPTH CALCULATIONS'//
                         .'  RANGE (FEET)        ECHO (SECONDS)         DEPTH (FEET)'//)
   ISN 0010      8        FORMAT (F6.0,F6.2)
   ISN 0011      9        FORMAT (T4,F6.0,T26,F4.2,T42,F6.0)
   ISN 0012               END
```

Figure 6.1

Page 4

```
          000000   47 F0 F 00C            MAIN  BC    15,12(0,15)

          000004   07404040                     DC    XL4'40404040'
          000008   40404040                     DC    XL4'40404040'
          00000C   90 EC D 00C                  STM   14,12,12(13)
          000010   98 23 F 020                  LM    2,3,32(15)
          000014   50 30 D 0C8                  ST    3,8(13)
          000018   50 D0 3 004                  ST    13,4(0,3)
          00001C   07 F2                        BCR   15,2

CONSTANTS
          0001C0   00000000                     DC    XL4'00000000'
          0001C4   00000002                     DC    XL4'00000002'
          0001C8   00001338                     DC    XL4'00001338'
          0001CC   00000000                     DC    XL4'00000000'
          000110   44133800                     DC    XL4'44133800'
          000114   41200000                     DC    XL4'41200000'
ADCONS FOR VARIABLES AND CONSTANTS
ADCONS FOR EXTERNAL REFERENCES
          000128   00000000                     DC    XL4'00000000'         SQRT
          00012C   00000000                     DC    XL4'00000000'         IBCOM#
          000138   58 F0 D 07C            1  L        15, 124( 0,13)        IBCOM#
          00013C   45 E0 F 004               BAL      14,   4( 0,15)
          000140   04000002                     DC    XL4'04000002'
          000144   00000028                     DC    XL4'00000028'         I%
          000148   45 E0 F 010               BAL      14,  16( 0,15)
          00014C   58 F0 D 07C            2  L        15, 124( 0,13)        IBCOM#
          000150   45 E0 F 000               BAL      14,   0( 0,15)
          000154   C4000001                     DC    XL4'C4000001'
          000158   00000093                     DC    XL4'00000093'         I
          00015C   45 E0 F 008               BAL      14,   8( 0,15)
          000160   04700068                     DC    XL4'04700068'         C
          000164   45 E0 F 008               BAL      14,   8( 0,15)
          000168   04700070                     DC    XL4'04700070'         T
          00016C   45 E0 F 010               BAL      14,  16( 0,15)
          000170   78 00 D 068            3  LE       0, 104( 0,13)         C
          000174   32 00                        LTER  0, 0
          000176   47 60 D 0D8                  BC    6, 216( 0,13)         4
          00017A   58 F0 D 07C       100001  L        15, 124( 0,13)        IBCOM#
          00017E   45 E0 F 034               BAL      14,  52( 0,15)
          000182   05                           DC    XL1'00000005'
          000183   40                           DC    XL1'00000040'
          000184   40                           DC    XL1'00000040'
          000185   40                           DC    XL1'00000040'
          000186   40                           DC    XL1'00000040'
          000187   F0                           DC    XL1'000000F0'
          000188   78 20 D 070            4  LE       2, 112( 0,13)         T
          00018C   7C 20 D 060               ME       2,  96( 0,13)         44133800
          000190   7D 20 D 064               DE       2, 100( 0,13)         41200000
          000194   3C 22                        MER   2, 2
```

Figure 6.1 (continued)

Page 5

```
         000196   78 40 D 068           LE     4, 104( 0,13)                C
         00019A   7D 40 D 064           DE     4, 100( 0,13)         412C0000
         00019E   3C 44                 MER    4, 4
         0001A0   3B 24                 SER    2, 4
         0001A2   7C 20 D 080           STE    2, 128( 0,13)             .TC0
         0001A6   41 10 D 04C           LA     1,  76( 0,13)
         0001AA   58 F0 D 078           L     15, 120( 0,13)             SQRT
         0001AE   05 EF                 BALR  14,15
         0001B0   70 00 D 084           STE    0, 132( 0,13)             .T01
         0001B4   78 00 D 084           LE     0, 132( 0,13)             .T01
         0001B8   7C 0C D 06C           STE    0, 108( 0,13)                D
         0001BC   58 FC D C7C     5     L     15, 124( 0,13)           IBCOM#
         0001C0   45 E0 F 004           BAL   14,   4( 0,15)
         0001C4   04000002              DC    XL4'04000002'
         0001C8   0000009B              DC    XL4'0000009B'
         0001CC   45 E0 F 008           BAL   14,   8( 0,15)
         0001D0   0470D068              DC    XL4'0470D068'                C
         0001D4   45 E0 F C08           BAL   14,   8( 0,15)
         0001D8   0470D070              DC    XL4'0470D070'                T
         0001DC   45 E0 F C08           BAL   14,   8( 0,15)
         0001E0   0470D06C              DC    XL4'0470D06C'                D
         0001E4   45 E0 F 010           BAL   14,  16( 0,15)
         0001E8   47 F0 D C9C     6     BC    15, 156( 0,13)                2
ADDRESS OF EPILOGUE
         0001EC   58 F0 D 07C           L     15, 124( 0,13)
         0001F0   45 E0 F 034           BAL   14,  52( 0,15)           IBCOM#
         0001F4   0540                  DC    XL2'40400540'
         0001F6   404040F0              DC    XL4'404040F0'
ADDRESS OF PROLOGUE
         0001FC   58 F0 3 07C           L     15, 124( 0, 3)
         000200   45 E0 F C40           BAL   14,  64( 0,15)           IBCOM#
         000204   18 D3                 LR    13, 3
         000206   47 F0 D 088           BC    15, 136( 0,13)
ADCON FOR PROLOGUE
         000020   000001FC              DC    XL4'000001FC'
ADCON FOR SAVE AREA
         000024   0CC000B0              DC    XL4'000000B0'
ADCON FOR EPILOGUE
         000080   000001EC              DC    XL4'000001EC'
ADCONS FOR PARAMETER LISTS
         0000FC   80000130              DC    XL4'80CC0130'             .TC0
ADCONS FOR TEMPORARIES
         000130   00000000              DC    XL4'00000000'
         000134   00C00000              DC    XL4'00000000'
ADCONS FOR 8 BLOCK LABELS

****** END OF COMPILATION ******
```

Figure 6.1 (continued)

Page 6

```
IEF285I    SYSOUT                                              SYSOUT
IEF285I    VOL SER NOS=      .
IEF285I    SYS68313.T105425.RP042.JDHABDC.R0000002              DELETED
IEF285I    VOL SER NOS=      .
IEF285I    SYS1.UT1                                             KEPT
IEF285I    VOL SER NOS= DCU1CO.
IEF285I    SYS68313.T105425.RP042.JDHABDC.R0000003              PASSED
IEF285I    VOL SER NOS= DCU1CO.
IEF285I    SYS68313.T105425.RP042.JDHABDC.R0000004              DELETED
IEF285I    VOL SER NOS= DCU1CO.
    **** TIME NOW= 10 HRS. 54 MIN. 30 SEC.    JOB= JDHABDC    STEP= FORT    ****
IEF236I ALLOC. FOR JDHABDC   LKED
IEF237I SYSLIB      ON 1C0
IEF237I             ON 292
IEF237I SYSLIN      ON 1C0
IEF237I SYSUT1      ON 1C0
IEF237I SYSLMOD     ON 1C0
```

Page 7

```
       E-LEVEL LINKAGE EDITOR OPTIONS SPECIFIED MAP
****MAIN       DOES NOT EXIST BUT HAS BEEN ADDED TO DATA SET


                                                     MODULE MAP

    CONTROL SECTION                     ENTRY

      NAME     ORIGIN    LENGTH           NAME     LOCATION     NAME     LOCATION

    MAIN         00        20A
    IHCSSQRT*   210         AC
                                         SQRT       210
    IHCFCOMH*   2C0        F20
                                         IBCOM#     2C0        FDIOCS#    37C
                                         CNTR1      E94        CNTR2      E98
                                         CNTR3      E9C        INTSW      10CC

    IHCUOPT *   11E0         8
    IHCTRCH *   11E8        2C8
    IHCFCVTH*   14B0       10A5
                                         ADCON#     14B0       FCVZO      15FC
                                         FCVAO      16A2       FCVLO      1732
                                         FCVIO      1A68       FCVEO      1F6A
                                         FCVCO      2184       INT6SW     2540

    IHCFIOSH*   2558        DA2
                                         FIOCS#     2558
    IHCUATBL*   3300        638
    IHCFINTH*   3938        4CE
                                         ARITH#     3938       ADJSW      3D11
    ENTRY ADDRESS             00
    TOTAL LENGTH             3E06
```

Figure 6.1 (continued)

164

Page 8

```
IEF285I    SYS1.FORTLIB                                    KEPT
IEF285I    VOL SER NOS= DCU1C0.
IEF285I    SYS1.CUCCLIB                                    KEPT
IEF285I    VOL SER NOS= DCU015.
IEF285I    SYS68313.T105425.RPC42.JDHABDC.R0000003         DELETED
IEF285I    VOL SER NOS= DCU1C0.
IEF285I    SYS1.UT1                                        KEPT
IEF285I    VOL SER NOS= DCU1C0.
IEF285I    GOSET                                           PASSED
IEF285I    VOL SER NOS= DCU1C0.
IEF285I    SYSOUT                                          SYSOUT
IEF285I    VOL SER NOS=           .
 ****  TIME NOW= 10 HRS. 54 MIN. 36 SEC.   JOB= JDHABDC   STEP= LKED    ****
IEF236I    ALLOC. FOR JDHABDC   GO
IEF237I    PGM=*.DD ON 1C0
IEF237I    FT05F001 ON 171
IEF237I    FT07F001 ON 173
IEF237I    FT01F001 ON 1C0
IEF237I    FT02F001 ON 291
IEF237I    FT03F001 ON 292
IEF237I    FT04F001 ON 292
```

Page 9

```
         ATALANTA - BEHEMOTH DEPTH CALCULATIONS

RANGE (FEET)       ECHO (SECONDS)       DEPTH (FEET)


    1000.              5.00                12290.
    5000.              5.00                12043.
    2000.              1.28                 2986.
```

Page 10

```
IEF285I    GOSET                                           PASSED
IEF285I    VOL SER NOS= DCU1C0.
IEF285I    SYSOUT                                          SYSOUT
IEF285I    VOL SER NOS=           .
IEF285I    SYS1.UT1                                        KEPT
IEF285I    VOL SER NOS= DCU1C0.
IEF285I    SYS1.UT2                                        KEPT
IEF285I    VOL SER NOS= DCU027.
IEF285I    SYS1.UT3                                        KEPT
IEF285I    VOL SER NOS= DCU015.
IEF285I    SYS1.UT4                                        KEPT
IEF285I    VOL SER NOS= DCU015.
 ****  TIME NOW= 10 HRS. 54 MIN. 38 SEC.   JOB= JDHABDC   STEP= GO      ****
IEF285I    GOSET                                           DELETED
IEF285I    VOL SER NOS= DCU1C0.
```

Figure 6.1 (continued)

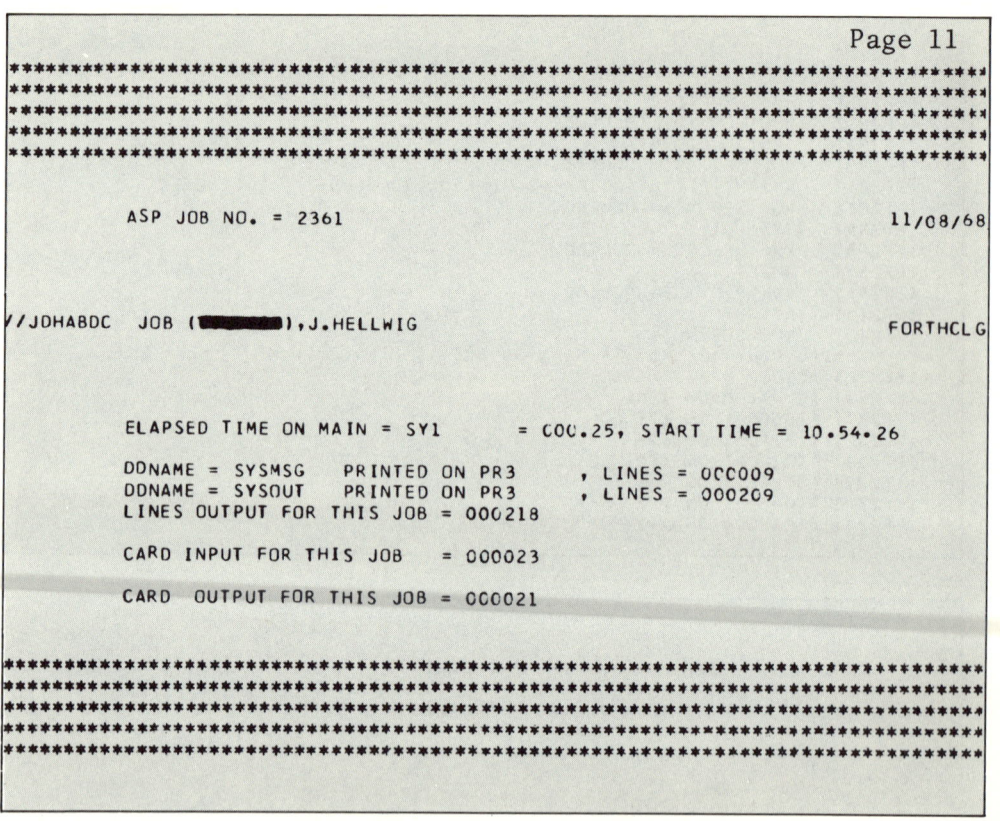

Figure 6.1 (concluded)

Clearly 'EXEC FORTHCLG' is an instance of impressive terseness. We'll get to the rest of the information on the EXEC card in a moment.

The operating system in the main processor (we'll call it OS/360, again for brevity's sake) has now read and interpreted the EXEC card. It gets ready to execute the first step, and prints (still on page 2) the message:

IEF236I ALLOC. FOR JDHABDC FORT

OS/360 messages are pretty esoteric; almost every one is preceded by a code number, like 'IEF236I,' which identifies the source and nature of the message. Should you ever want to know what one of these messages means, you can look it up in an OS/360 manual, where the messages and their interpretations are filed according to the code number.

This particular message indicates that OS/360 is getting ready ('allocating its resources') for the first step -- FORT -- of job JDHABDC. The rest of the messages on page 2 have to do with this allocation of resources -- which in this case are I/O devices. This information is of no interest to the programmer unless something very unusual goes wrong with his program or the system.

Page 3 is more interesting. Here is the beginning of the output of the FORTRAN compiler. Between pages 2 and 3 control has been given by OS/360 to the compiler, and the first step is being carried out. The compiler announces itself by telling us which of several possible compilers it is. This is the 'H' version, implemented January 1, 1968. Going back to the EXEC card for a moment: if we had said 'EXEC FORTGCLG', we would have asked for the 'G' version of the compiler. The reasons for picking one rather than the other are beyond the scope of this discussion.

Next on page 3 is a message that begins

COMPILER OPTIONS -

with two lines of words separated by commas. There are certain options available to a programmer using the compiler. For example, he may choose to have an object deck punched, or not.

If he wants a deck, he can put on the EXEC card:

    // EXEC   FORTHCLG,PARM.FORT='DECK'

whereas if he does not want one, he can write:

    // EXEC   FORTHCLG,PARM.FORT='NODECK'

where 'PARM.FORT' means 'parameters (options) for the FORT step.'

Another option is 'LIST' or 'NOLIST', where one asks the compiler to (or not to) print out a list of the compiled machine-code instructions for the program. If you look back at the EXEC card used for this job, you can see that we asked for a list and a deck. We also provided a parameter for the LKED, or linkage editor step; we shall see what that means shortly.

For each of the available options, the compiler has a *default* condition, which is what you get if you don't ask for anything. In the Columbia system, NODECK and NOLIST are defaults. Following the words 'COMPILER OPTIONS' on page 3 is a list of all the possible options as they have been selected for this job. We could have given the program a name; since we did not (we gave the *job* a name, but that's different) it gets the default name 'MAIN'. 'DECK' and 'LIST' were explicitly requested; all the others are shown in their default status. What they all mean is not very important at this point.

The compiler reads the source statements, and as it does so it performs the first stage of the translation process. In the course of scanning a single statement at a time, it can recognize what kind of statement each one is. After the scan is completed, the statement is printed. If there are errors in the syntax of any statement, the compiler can print a diagnostic immediately following the erroneous statement. (In the present example there are no errors.) After all the source statements have been read, the compiler proceeds to generate the object program. In the course of doing so, it may find more errors -- errors in the syntax of the program as a whole.

On the left margin of the listing are statement identifiers created by the compiler, called *internal statement numbers* (ISN's). The statement numbers assigned by the programmer --

called *external statement numbers* -- are required only when the programmer needs to refer to a statement in the program. The compiler -- as well as other parts of the system -- occasionally needs a way to refer to a statement, so it generates its own reference numbers.

If you examine the ISN's, you will notice first of all that they start at ISN 0002. The compiler uses the internal number 1 for mysterious purposes of its own. Next, you will notice that 5 is missing. That is because the 'IF' statement is a compound. This kind of 'IF' can have almost any legitimate statement as its second part; it is not restricted to STOP. Thus the compiler must analyze the second part to see what kind of statement it is; in the process it gives it a number. ISN0004 is assigned to the first part, and ISN0005 to the second.

On the other hand, the compiler recognizes that the FORMAT statement with external number 7 (ISN0009) is only one statement, even though it takes up two cards.

Page 4 is the beginning of the list of compiled object code, as requested by the compiler option 'LIST'. Most of pages 4 and 5 is incomprehensible except to someone familiar with 360 instruction code. Furthermore, it is rarely necessary for anyone to see what the object code looks like; that is why the compiler option has the default 'NOLIST.' It is worthwhile to look at an *object listing* once, however, just to get an idea of what goes on.

Beginning with the first line on page 4: the first code in the program is an instruction. Coded in hexadecimal, this instruction reads:

                47 F0 F 00C

where each hexadecimal character represents four bits, or a half-byte. The instruction is thus four bytes long. You may recall that 360 memory is divided into registers, each holding one byte of information. This instruction will thus occupy four memory registers.

In the object listing, all compiled instructions and data are numbered sequentially by bytes, starting at zero. The

numbers appear to the left of the object code itself. The
first instruction is assigned numbers 000000 through 000003,
but only the lowest number is actually printed out. As you
can see, the next line is numbered 000004. The compiled code
in the second line,

        07404040

is also four bytes long, and gets numbers 000004 through 000007.
And, naturally, the third line begins at number 000008. This
counting, alas, is done in hexadecimal, so from here on it is
confusing to follow.

    There is, then, a column of information lined up under the
first instruction, '47 F0 F 00C,' which is the actual compiled
program. All the rest of the information on pages 4 and 5 --
the numbers to the left and all the printing to the right of
this column -- is explanatory material. What is on the right
is a recoding of the object code into something like the symbolic machine language that was described in Chapters 1 and 3.

    There are some comprehensible parts. Let us divide the
listing into five columns. The first two we have already iden-
tified: the byte-number, or relative-address column, and the
object-code column. The third column has very few entries and
is called the symbolic-address column; the first-line entry in
this column is the word 'MAIN.' The first entry in the fourth
column is

        BC   15,12(0,15)

and it is called the symbolic-instruction column. The fifth,
the symbolic-reference column, has no entry in the first line.
Halfway down the page is the first line with an entry, 'SQRT.'

    The symbolic addresses, where they appear, identify the
beginnings of sections of code. We observed earlier that the
program had been given the default name MAIN; this name identifies the beginning of the program. Looking down this column,
you will see the numbers 1, 2, 3, 4, 5, and 6 (there is also a
number 100001, which does not concern us here). These numbers
correspond to the *external* statement numbers used by the programmer. They mark the beginning of the machine code generated

for each FORTRAN statement. If you want to look at the code generated for statement number 4, you look for '4' in the symbolic-address column.

Why are there no entries for statements 7, 8, and 9 of the source program? The answer is that these statements are of a different sort from the others. They are not imperatives, like the rest of the statements. They supply auxiliary information -- specifically, they describe the format of input or output data -- rather than the actions to be performed. As a result, they do not give rise to machine instructions, but are treated more like data. They do not, in this example, appear in the object listing at all.

Locate the line of code with relative address (byte number) 000188. It reads as follows:

    000188   78 20 D 070   4   LE   2, 112(0,13)   T

The entry in the object-code column is an instruction, '78 20 D 070', which can be paraphrased as "get the word stored at location D070 and load it into register 2." The symbolic address of this instruction is 4, which means it is the first instruction in the code generated for FORTRAN statement number 4. The symbolic form of this instruction:

        LE   2, 112(0,13)

is not very helpful. But in the symbolic-reference column we find T, which is very helpful indeed. That is the source-program name for the item that the instruction refers to -- the item that is being fetched from memory.

Statement 4 reads

      D = SQRT ((4920 * T/2)**2 - (C/2)**2)

When this computation is carried out -- by computer or by a human being -- it is done in the following order, or a slight variation thereof:

        get the value of T;

        multiply it by 4920;

        divide the result by 2;

square the result;

save this number;

get the value of C;

divide it by 2;

square the result;

subtract this number from the one you saved before;

take the square root of the result;

that is the value of D.

Consequently, the first compiled instruction corresponding to statement 4 is, as it should be, 'Get T.' The next line down reads

    00018C 7C 20 D 060   ME   2,   96(0,13)   44133800

which amounts to 'Multiply by 4920.' The symbolic-reference column is supposed to tell us what we are multiplying by. It does, in that 44133800 is what 4920 looks like when it is converted to hexadecimal floating-point.

    Most FORTRAN programmers do not make use of the object listing of their program. Many, in fact, do not know how to interpret it. It is useful, however, to know that the object listing exists and to have a general idea of what it consists of. On to page 6.

    Page 6 consists of messages from OS/360, because the compiler is all through. OS does some cleaning up between steps, prints some incomprehensible messages, and then (about two-thirds of the way down) announces the end of the FORT job step by giving the time. The next line is the now familiar 'allocation' message that heralds the beginning of the second job step, LKED. The rest of 6 is uninteresting.

    What does a linkage editor do? It prepares your program for execution, by creating what may be called a *load module*. It knows better than you what needs to be done for you. It knows what library subprograms are required, and that they must know where, in memory, to find each other. The load module is all the necessary programs, set up to communicate with each other, and all ready to be slipped into memory and executed.

Page 7 shows the layout of the load module. This would not normally be printed. We have it here as a result of saying PARM.LKED='MAP' on the EXEC card. This is one of several programmer options defined by the linkage editor.

Under the heading 'CONTROL SECTION' are three columns: NAME, ORIGIN, and LENGTH. The linkage editor has looked at the compiled object program for ABDC -- called MAIN -- and put it first in the load module. The linkage editor assigns tentative memory locations to everything. It says, in effect, "Let's suppose we put MAIN at location zero. It's 20A bytes long (counting in hexadecimal, as usual). It needs the SQRT program -- let's put that starting at location 210. Then where can we put the next program?" And so forth. The *origin* of a program is simply where it begins in this scheme.

So there on page 7 is MAIN, at origin zero. IHCSSQRT* is the square-root program in disguise. The main program does reading and printing, and these are handled by a subprogram called IHCFCOMH*. (All of these subprograms are brought in from the system library in secondary storage.) This program, IHCFCOMH*, itself calls upon a whole series of other library subprograms. These come next: IHCUOPT*, IHCTRCH*, and so forth, down to the last one, IHCFINTH*. The total length of this whole collection -- the resulting load module -- is 3E06 bytes. The decimal equivalent of 3E06 is 15,878.

On the right side of the page, under the heading 'ENTRY,' are the locations of key addresses in the subprograms that have been loaded. These are the addresses to which other programs will refer. They represent the interprogram communication links that it is the linkage editor's job to set up.

Page 8 is very like page 6, and shows the transition from the second step, LKED, to the third, GO. By comparing the times on pages 6 and 8 you can see that the LKED step took 6 seconds.

The linkage editor has created an executable load module, which it has actually written out on secondary storage. At the beginning of the GO step, the OS/360 control program brings this load module into main memory and gives it control. It is worth noting here that the control program decides where in memory the load module is to go. It may go one place one day, and another the next. Programs must thus be written so that they make no assumptions about the *absolute* memory locations available to them. This is of no concern to the FORTRAN programmer, however; the compiler automatically creates location-independent programs.

Page 9, rather anticlimactically, shows the output of the main program itself. There is our title, and there are our column headings, input data values, and results, just as we asked for them.

Page 10 has the usual incomprehensible interstep messages. By comparing the times on pages 8 and 10, we can see that execution of the object program took 2 seconds.

Page 11, the last page of the output, is written by ASP in the support processor. The job has left the main processor, and ASP now presents final statistics for the job. The total time spent in the main processor was 0.25 minute, or 15 seconds. The job went to the main processor at 10:54:26. If we look back at the time on page 6, we note that the FORT step was finished at 10:54:30, so it took 4 seconds. Four seconds to compile, six for the linkage editor, and two to execute adds up to twelve seconds. Have we been cheated?

Not really. The extra few seconds are attributable to an invisible but persistent phenomenon called *system overhead*, which exists, to a greater or lesser degree, in any operating system. In the first place, the operating system has some cleaning up to do after each job. There is some time, then, between the termination of the last job step and the termination of the job as a whole. Second, the fact that there are two processors in this system can explain part of the discrepancy. The time messages at the conclusion of each job step are generated by the main processor, whereas the message

```
ELAPSED TIME ON MAIN = SY1 = 000.25
```

is based on time computed by the support processor. When the main processor 'clocks off' a job, some cleaning-up time is required on the part of the support processor before the next job can be initiated. Finally, when the support processor initiates a new job, it must devote some time to preparing it to run on the main processor; this time is charged to the new job. The time for these three system functions -- one in OS, two in ASP -- is included in the total job time. Note, however, that the user is not being charged here for support processor time; he is charged, rather, for any time during which the main processor has to wait for the support processor.

   Although in this example the overhead is a large percentage of the total job time, this is simply due to the fact that the total job time is so small. A long-running job will probably experience a similar amount -- hence a smaller percentage -- of system overhead time.

EXERCISES

6.1   If the following message appeared on the output of job ABDC:

   ERROR AT ISN 0006

   THE EXPRESSION HAS AT LEAST ONE TOO FEW RIGHT PARENTHESES

to which statement would you look for the source of the error?

6.2   In the object listing for ABDC, find the byte numbers (relative addresses) of the instruction that fetches the value of C from memory to test if it is equal to zero.

Check your answers before going on.

175

3. *Checking the Results*

Probably the most important thing that computer users must do is to verify that computer-generated results are correct. The first few times a program is run, there are usually obvious bugs to be eliminated. Once these have been solved, the program should be run with test input data for the purpose of verifying the results in some manner. The results of the ABDC program, for example, give values of the ocean depth for three pairs of values for ship range and echo time. It would be suitable for these three calculations to be checked by hand.

In some cases, of course, it may be impossible to check final results by hand. The major reason for using the computer may be just that the computation is too complex to be carried out by people in a reasonable amount of time. There are two methods that should be applied, in this case, to the control of errors. The first is, simply to know a reasonable result from an unreasonable one, and to judge all final results on this basis. The second is to rely on what is called 'modular programming.' A complex problem is broken down into component subproblems. Each of these is coded as a separate subprogram, and each is tested independently, with special test data. If each 'module' can be trusted, this increases the probability that when they are combined the net results will be reliable. Any problem of complexity, in fact, should be broken up in this fashion into a collection of subprograms.

If the results are correct, the program can be put into production status and used to process large amounts of data. The same program may be used every time a new set of data is obtained. Because it worked on test data, we can assume that it will work on real data. But it is also important that production results be monitored constantly. They should always be examined for 'reasonableness,' as a safeguard against obscure errors that may not have shown up in the tests and against changes and errors in the computer system that might affect the validity of the results.

There are many possible causes of error that should make programmers constantly suspicious. The one that may come first to mind is the machine itself. Generally speaking it is safe to assume that the computer does not make errors, although there are hardware failures that can produce wrong results. This is doubly rare, however: first, because computer hardware is reliable and is continually checked for reliability; second, because a hardware failure is more likely to cause obvious problems -- such as the inability of the computer operators to get the system going at all, or the complete failure of a job to go through -- than to cause such an unobtrusive error as a wrong answer.

Consequently the hardware is probably the element to suspect last. There is another reason for this, too. It is extremely difficult to identify the origin of a hardware failure, unless it is consistent and gives rise to reproducible errors. Isolating an obscure transient hardware error is a task so near to hopelessness that it should be attempted only when it is clear that no other source of error can be found.

The next place you might be tempted to look is in the software. Although software errors are not rare, they also tend to be fairly obvious. They may cause your program to produce ridiculous results, or none at all. Software programs are usually tested very thoroughly, and errors usually result from their complexity rather than from any sloppiness on the part of their authors.

What it comes down to, then, is that if your results are wrong, it is probably your program that is at fault. At any rate, there is the first place to look. If you do have bad results, there are techniques for isolating the error that have been developed over the years. They fall into two categories: ways of programming that build tests into a program from the beginning; and ways of modifying a bad program to find out what went wrong. The former type is more successful, in the long run.

EXERCISE 6.3

Figure 6.2 shows another version of the ABDC program, and the results it produced. They are different from the ones in Figure 6.1. Is there anything about either set of results to make you suspicious? Which program is correct? Why is the wrong one wrong?

Check your answer before going on.

```
                                                                    Page 1
ISN 0002    1       PRINT 7
ISN 0003    2       READ 8, C, T
ISN 0004    3       IF (C .EQ. 0) STOP
ISN 0006    4       D = SQRT ((4920 * T/2)**2 - (C/2))
ISN 0007    5       PRINT 9, C, T, D
ISN 0008    6       GO TO 2
ISN 0009    7       FORMAT ('1         ATALANTA - BEHEMOTH DEPTH CALCULATIONS'//
                   .' RANGE (FEET)         ECHO (SECONDS)         DEPTH (FEET)'///)
ISN 0010    8       FORMAT (F6.0,F6.2)
ISN 0011    9       FORMAT (T4,F6.0,T26,F4.2,T42,F6.0)
ISN 0012            END
```

```
                                                                    Page 2
             ATALANTA - BEHEMOTH DEPTH CALCULATIONS
   RANGE (FEET)         ECHO (SECONDS)         DEPTH (FEET)


        1000.                5.00                12300.
        5000.                5.00                12300.
        2000.                1.28                 3149.
```

Figure 6.2

178

4. *System Diagnostics: Compiler Messages*

One of the most important functions of an operating system is to monitor user programs and apply some control of errors. A large class of programmer errors, or probable errors, can be detected by the system.

We have already seen, in passing, one of the ways the system detects a 'probable' error: if a program runs longer than the user says it should, his time estimate may be wrong; but it is more likely that his program is not doing what it is supposed to do. If a program has accidentally been coded as an infinite loop, for example, it will, in principle, run forever. The operating system, by terminating a job when its time estimate has been exceeded, protects the user from charges for excessive computer time.

Each program in the system -- control program, translator, or library subprogram -- checks the validity of the input information it receives. The control program checks control cards, the compiler checks source statements, and library subprograms check the input values transmitted to them. Responsibility for checking the validity of data input to the user program lies, clearly, with the user. To some extent, however, the system can help here, too. Since, in FORTRAN, reading and writing of data are actually carried out by library subprograms, these routines can detect some potential sources of error in the input data.

The sample programs developed in this text do not perform any checking, but they should do so. One of the most effective checks that can be built into a program that processes numerical data, for example, consists of defining the range of possible values for each input variable. Each input value is then checked against this range; if it lies outside, the program can reject the data and print a diagnostic message. The programmer, while designing a program, must always be conscious of how erroneous or simply unusual input values may affect the logical flow of the program.

System programs generally have two ways of dealing with errors. If the error is apparently severe, the job or job step can be terminated; in this case an explanatory message will be

printed on the output listing. If the error is apparently
minor, a warning message can be printed, and execution of the
job can be continued. Errors are assumed to be severe if they
really prevent the program from doing its job; for example, a
nonsense statement encountered by the FORTRAN compiler prevents
it from generating a meaningful translation. Errors may also be
judged severe if there is a reasonable probability that they will
cause trouble later, either for the programmer or for the system
as a whole.

Let's look at some specific errors, and at how the Columbia
ASP/OS system dealt with them. Figure 6.3 shows another attempt
to run the ABDC program. Only a few pages of the output are
shown -- those that reflect the errors made in this version of
the program. The first page shows the listing of the source
program. The second page contains 'FORTRAN H ERROR MESSAGES,'
and the third page shows the OS/360 messages that always appear
between the job steps.

There are several error conditions noted here. First,
there is an interlinear comment following statement number 3 on
the first page. It tells us there is something wrong with the
third statement, but it is not very helpful. The 'SCAN POINTER'
will sometimes give valuable information about where in the
statement the error appears, but in this case it isn't much
good.

On the second page are some helpful diagnostics. The first
says: "At ISN 0005 there is an error; it is OS/360 recognizable
error number IEK036I, and it is of severity level 8." There
follows an explanation of the error. Severity levels are ranked
so that the worse the error, the higher the number: eight is
pretty bad, and the program is going to be rejected.

Now, as we noted earlier, ISN0005 does not appear on the
source listing but is assigned to the second part of the IF
statement. How could we have committed invalid syntax on such
a simple statement as 'STOP'? Well, if you look very carefully
at the source listing, you will see that the third character is
zero, not 'oh.' To the compiler, the two characters do not
look at all alike; one looks like '11110000', while the other
is '11010110'. There is just no way for the compiler to guess

```
                                                                Page 1
    ISN 0002      1      PRINT 7
    ISN 0003      2      READ 8, C, T
    ISN 0004      3      IF (C .EQ. 0) STOP
ERROR DETECTED - SCAN POINTER =    1
    ISN 0006      4      D = SRQT ((4920 * T/2)**2 - (C/2)**2)
    ISN 0007      5      PRINT 9, C, T, D
    ISN 0008      6      GO TO 12
    ISN 0009      7      FORMAT ('1        ATALANTA - BEHEMOTH DEPTH CALCULATIONS'//
                         .'   RANGE (FEET)         ECHO (SECONDS)        DEPTH (FEET)'//)
    ISN 0010      8      FORMAT (F6.0,F6.2)
    ISN 0011      9      FORMAT (T4,F6.0,T26,F4.2,T42,F6.0)
    ISN 0012     10      END
```

```
                                              FORTRAN H ERROR MESSAGES   Page 2

                ERROR NO    LEVEL      ERROR MESSAGE


    ISN   0005   IEK036I      8        THE STATEMENT CONTAINS INVALID SYNTAX.
                                       THE STATEMENT CANNOT BE CLASSIFIED.


    ISN   0012   IEK225I      4        A LABEL APPEARS ON A NON-EXECUTABLE
                                       STATEMENT. THE LABEL IS IGNORED.


    LABEL 000012 IEK332I      8        THE STATEMENT NUMBER IS UNDEFINED.



****** END OF COMPILATION ******
```

```
    IEF285I    SYS69124.T230105.RV000.JDHTRY1.R0000038       DELETED    Page 3
    IEF285I    VOL SER NOS=        .
    IEF285I    SYS69124.T230105.RV000.JDHTRY1.R0000039       DELETED
    IEF285I    VOL SER NOS= DRM291.
    IEF285I    SYS69124.T230105.RV000.JDHTRY1.R0000040       DELETED
    IEF285I    VOL SER NOS= DRM191.
    IEF285I    SYS69124.T230105.RV000.JDHTRY1.R0000041       PASSED
    IEF285I    VOL SER NOS= DRM291.
     ** TIME NOW= 23 HRS. 27 MIN. 50 SEC.        JOB= JDHTRY1    STEP= FORT
    IEF202I - STEP - LKED   , WAS NOT RUN BECAUSE OF CONDITION CODES.
    IEF236I ALLOC. FOR JDHTRY1   LKED
     ** TIME NOW= 23 HRS. 27 MIN. 53 SEC.        JOB= JDHTRY1    STEP= LKED
    IEF202I - STEP - GO     , WAS NOT RUN BECAUSE OF CONDITION CODES.
    IEF236I ALLOC. FOR JDHTRY1   GO
     ** TIME NOW= 23 HRS. 28 MIN. 04 SEC.        JOB= JDHTRY1    STEP= GO
    IEF285I    SYS69124.T230105.RV000.JDHTRY1.R0000041       DELETED
    IEF285I    VOL SER NOS= DRM291.
```

Figure 6.3

what was intended.*

The next error message concerns ISN0012, the 'END' statement. In this version of ABDC, the END statement has been given a label (statement number) and the compiler observes that there is no point in putting a label on a statement to which control can <u>never</u> be transferred. This is an example of the compiler being rather picayune. It ignores the label, however, and gives the error a severity level of only 4; this would not cause the program to be rejected if there were no higher-level error.

Interpretation of the third error message, of severity level 8 like the first, is left as an exercise for the reader. On the last page of Figure 6.3, we find out what OS/360 has done about the steps of this job. The FORT step has been completed, but it has transmitted to OS/360, by a medium known as the 'condition code,' the fact that severe errors were found. The control program, on the basis of this information, decides that executing the LKED and GO steps would be a waste of time. Messages are printed to inform the user that these steps were not run, and the job is terminated.

As with most system decisions, the user can, if he wishes, override this judgment. Specifying his intentions on the appropriate control cards, he can, in effect, say that he wants to go on even if errors are encountered. This request will be honored up to a point; but the system will try not to allow him to do anything that will adversely affect other users in the system.

---

*   There are ways, actually, to make computer programs, and translators in particular, more 'understanding.' These techniques are expensive, however, in that they increase the amount of computer time required to translate a program. Permissive compilers are in the same philosophical and economic camp as interactive terminal systems.

EXERCISE 6.4

What is the cause of the third error message on the second page of Figure 6.3? Note that by 'LABEL' FORTRAN means 'external statement number,' not 'ISN.'

Check your answer before going on.

5. *System Diagnostics: Linkage Editor and Library Messages*

Figure 6.4 shows what happened when the severe errors detected by the compiler, shown in Figure 6.3, were corrected and the job was run again. On the first page is the source listing. The FORTRAN error messages (which are indicated as Page 2 in the figure) consist only of the warning about the END statement. Since this is a low-severity error, the FORT step is regarded as successful. After the usual interstep messages (not shown here) control was transferred to the linkage editor, output from which is shown (slightly edited) on the second page of the figure (indicated as Page 3).

Here another type of error has been encountered, and a severe one, at that. The linkage editor has been told that the user program needs a library subprogram named SRQT (see statement 4 of the source listing.) The linkage editor searches the system library in vain for a routine with this name. SQRT, yes; but SRQT is not there, and the linkage editor is not designed to recognize any similarity between these two strings of characters. The module map is shown without any entry for a square-root routine, and the linkage editor informs the control program that a high-severity error has been found.

Following this (indicated as Page 4) is the OS/360 interstep information. The LKED step is completed, and then the GO step is suppressed and the job terminated.

In Figure 6.5 the misspelling of SQRT has been corrected, and the job resubmitted. (The extraneous statement number was removed, too.) Everything was normal, with no diagnostic messages in the output of the FORT or LKED steps, and the results (indicated as Page 2 in the figure) were identical to those of Figure 6.1. The only difference between the two jobs, in fact, was that more input data values were provided, added into the deck just after the original ones.

Following the correct results for the first three sets of input data is a series of diagnostic messages that are about as mysterious as you'll find. The obscurity of OS/360 diagnostics is pretty severe in general, and particularly bad for errors encountered during the execution of the user's program (the GO

```
ISN 0002    1     PRINT 7                                                    Page 1
ISN 0003    2     READ 8, C, T
ISN 0004    3     IF (C .EQ. 0) STOP
ISN 0006    4     D = SRQT ((4920 * T/2)**2 - (C/2)**2)
ISN 0007    5     PRINT 9, C, T, D
ISN 0008    6     GO TO 2
ISN 0009    7     FORMAT ('1         ATALANTA - BEHEMOTH DEPTH CALCULATIONS'//
                  .' RANGE (FEET)         ECHO (SECONDS)         DEPTH (FEET)'///)
ISN 0010    8     FORMAT (F6.0,F6.2)
ISN 0011    9     FORMAT (T4,F6.0,T26,F4.2,T42,F6.0)
ISN 0012   10     END
```

```
                                                                    Page 2


                                        FORTRAN H ERROR MESSAGES

              ERROR NO    LEVEL         ERROR MESSAGE

   ISN    0012   IEK225I      4         A LABEL APPEARS ON A NON-EXECUTABLE
                                        STATEMENT. THE LABEL IS IGNORED.
****** END OF COMPILATION ******
```

Figure 6.4

```
IEW0132  SRQT                                                            Page 3
                                             MODULE MAP
     CONTROL SECTION              ENTRY
      NAME    ORIGIN  LENGTH        NAME    LOCATION      NAME    LOCATION

     MAIN        00     20E
     IHCECOMH*  210     FF1
                                  IBCOM#      210       FDIOCS#     2CC
     IHCCOMH2* 1208     3F0
                                  SEQDASD    1320
     IHCFCVTH* 1608    1160
                                  ADCON#     1608       FCVAOUTP   1682
                                  FCVIOUTP   1C1E       FCVEOUTP   2120
     IHCEFNTH* 2778     562
                                  ARITH#     2778       ADJSWTCH   2B34
     IHCEFIOS* 2CE0    1100
                                  FIOCS#     2CE0       FIOCSREP   2CE6
     IHCUOPT * 3DE0     320
     IHCERRM * 4100     59C
                                  ERRMON     4100       IHCERRE    4118
     IHCUATBL* 46A0     638
     IHCETRCH* 4CD8     28E
                                  IHCTRCH    4CD8       ERRTRA     4CE0

     ENTRY ADDRESS       00
     TOTAL LENGTH      4F68

  ****MAIN     DOES NOT EXIST BUT HAS BEEN ADDED TO DATA SET
  **MODULE HAS BECOME NOT EXECUTABLE

                                              DIAGNOSTIC MESSAGE DIRECTORY

     IEW0132 ERROR - SYMBOL PRINTED IS AN UNRESOLVED EXTERNAL REFERENCE.
```

```
                                                                         Page 4
     IEF285I    SYS1.FORTLIB                             KEPT
     IEF285I    VOL SER NOS= DRM291.
     IEF285I    SYS1.CUCCLIB                             KEPT
     IEF285I    VOL SER NOS= DCU015.
     IEF285I    SYS69124.T230105.RV000.JDHTRY2.R0000055  DELETED
     IEF285I    VOL SER NOS=           .
     IEF285I    SYS69124.T230105.RV000.JDHTRY2.GOSET     PASSED
     IEF285I    VOL SER NOS= DRM191.
     IEF285I    SYS69124.T230105.RV000.JDHTRY2.R0000056  DELETED
     IEF285I    VOL SER NOS= DRM191.
     IEF285I    SYS69124.T230105.RV000.JDHTRY2.R0000054  DELETED
     IEF285I    VOL SER NOS= DCU119.
     ** TIME NOW= 23 HRS. 28 MIN. 13 SEC.        JOB= JDHTRY2   STEP= LKED
     IEF202I - STEP - GO     , WAS NOT RUN BECAUSE OF CONDITION CODES.
     IEF236I ALLOC. FOR JDHTRY2   GO
     ** TIME NOW= 23 HRS. 28 MIN. 17 SEC.        JOB= JDHTRY2   STEP= GO
     IEF285I    SYS69124.T230105.RV000.JDHTRY2.GOSET     DELETED
     IEF285I    VOL SER NOS= DRM191.
```

Figure 6.4 (concluded)

step). Other operating systems have done better in this respect, and future systems should do better. Still, like anything else, it's all in knowing how. Here the crucial piece of information is the OS/360 code number, IHC251I. In this case the rest of the information can be ignored.

Armed with this number, the programmer can go to an OS/360 manual that lists all error codes in alphabetic and numeric order. Under the entry IHC251I he will find the following explanation:

> "In the subprogram IHCSSQRT (SQRT), the argument is less than zero."

In other words, the value transmitted to the SQRT program was negative; SQRT regards an attempt to take the square root of a negative number as illegitimate. When this condition arises, the SQRT program informs the control program that the program should be terminated.

The programmer, encountering this condition, now looks at his input data. He can assume that the trouble was caused by the fourth input data card, since the first three were printed out correctly. In this case, the fourth data card looked like this:

> 5000.   1.00

that is, a value of 5000 feet for the range, and one second for the echo. A quick estimate shows that with these values the expression

> (4920*T/2)**2 - (C/2)**2

is indeed negative. Consideration of the physical situation that gave rise to the equation will establish that those input values must be wrong, since they describe a physical impossibility. With the two ships 5000 feet apart, the echo *must* take more than a second to arrive.

```
ISN 0002     1     PRINT 7
ISN 0003     2     READ 8, C, T
ISN 0004     3     IF (C .EQ. 0) STOP
ISN 0006     4     D = SQRT (((4920 * T/2)**2 - (C/2)**2)
ISN 0007     5     PRINT 9, C, T, D
ISN 0008     6     GO TO 2
ISN 0009     7     FORMAT ('1         ATALANTA - BEHEMOTH DEPTH CALCULATIONS'//
                  .' RANGE (FEET)        ECHO (SECONDS)        DEPTH (FEET)'//)
ISN 0010     8     FORMAT (F6.0,F6.2)
ISN 0011     9     FORMAT (T4,F6.0,T26,F4.2,T42,F6.0)
ISN 0012           END
```

```
            ATALANTA - BEHEMOTH DEPTH CALCULATIONS

     RANGE (FEET)        ECHO (SECONDS)        DEPTH (FEET)


         1000.                5.00                12290.
         5000.                5.00                12043.
         2000.                1.28                 2986.

  IHC251I

  TRACEBACK FOLLOWS-    ROUTINE      ISN    REG. 14

                         MAIN               C0C04D9C

  ENTRY POINT=  70025020
```

Figure 6.5

6. *A Final Illustration*

Figure 6.6 shows the complete printed output for the job GEOM, run under the Columbia University ASP/OS system as described earlier.

Since the EXEC card mentioned no special options, all the default options for FORT and LKED have been used. Thus the object deck was omitted, as well as the compiler object listing and the linkage editor module map.

The sum of the series

$$R + R^2 + \ldots + R^n$$

approaches the value $R/(1-R)$ as N, the number of terms included in the sum, increases. Thus for $R = 0.5$, the sum should approach 1. The output of Figure 6.6 shows that, for this value of R, the sum is very close to the limit when N is equal to 30.

For $R = 0.9$, the sum approaches 9. It is apparent from the result of the test job, however, that the sum approaches its limit (converges) more slowly for this value of R. Even with fifty terms, it is not very close yet.

```
                                                                    Page 1
//JDHGEOM   JOB (▆▆▆▆▆),J.HELLWIG
//   EXEC   FORTHCLG
//FORT.SYSIN DD *
/*
//GO.SYSIN DD *
/*
R=IHC002I STOP      0
R=IEC202I K 171,
R=IEF161I READER CLOSED
```

```
                                                                    Page 2
//JDHGEOM   JOB (▆▆▆▆▆),J.HELLWIG
IEF236I ALLOC. FOR JDHGEOM    FORT
IEF237I SYSPUNCH ON 173
IEF237I SYSUT1   ON 1C0
IEF237I SYSLIN   ON 1C0
IEF237I SYSUT2   ON 1C0
IEF237I SYSIN    ON 171
```

```
                                                                    Page 3

LEVEL 15 ( 1 JAN 68)                              OS/360   FORTRAN H

        COMPILER OPTIONS - NAME=  MAIN,OPT=C2,LINECNT=5C,SOURCE,EBCDIC,
                          NOLIST,NODECK,LOAD,NOMAP,NOEDIT,NOID,NOXREF


    ISN 0002            PRINT 13
    ISN 0C03      2     READ 14,R,N
    ISN 0004            IF (R .EQ. 0) STOP
    ISN 0006            T=1
    ISN 0C07            S=0
    ISN 0008            I=1
    ISN 0009      7     T=T*R
    ISN 001C            S=S+T
    ISN C011            I=I+1
    ISN 0C12            IF (I .LE. N) GO TO 7
    ISN 0014            PRINT 15,R,N,S
    ISN 0015            GO TO 2
    ISN 0C16      13    FORMAT ('1    GEOMETRIC SERIES'//
                       .'   BASE     NO. TERMS      SUM'//)
    ISN 0C17      14    FORMAT (F5.2,I5)
    ISN 0018      15    FORMAT (F7.2,I9,6X,F11.8)
    ISN 0C19            END

****** END OF COMPILATION ******
```

Figure 6.6

```
                                                          Page 4
IEF285I    SYSOUT                                SYSOUT
IEF285I    VOL SER NOS=
IEF285I    SYS1.UT1                              KEPT
IEF285I    VOL SER NOS= DCU1C0.
IEF285I    SYS68313.T105806.RPO44.JDHGEOM.R0OC0C03   PASSED
IEF285I    VOL SER NOS= DCU1C0.
IEF285I    SYS68313.T105806.RPC44.JDHGEOM.ROCOC0O4   DELETED
IEF285I    VOL SER NOS= DCU1CC.
 **** TIME NOW= 10 HRS. 58 MIN. 11 SEC.   JOB= JDHGEOM   STEP= FORT    ****
IEF236I ALLOC. FOR JDHGEOM   LKED
IEF237I SYSLIB       ON 1C0
IEF237I              ON 292
IEF237I SYSLIN       ON 1C0
IEF237I SYSUT1       ON 1C0
IEF237I SYSLMOD      ON 1C0
```

```
                                                          Page 5



   E-LEVEL LINKAGE EDITOR OPTIONS SPECIFIED LIST
 ****MAIN         DOES NOT EXIST BUT HAS BEEN ADDED TO DATA SET
```

```
                                                          Page 6
IEF285I    SYS1.FORTLIB                          KEPT
IEF285I    VOL SER NOS= DCU1C0.
IEF285I    SYS1.CUCCLIB                          KEPT
IEF285I    VOL SER NOS= DCU015.
IEF285I    SYS68313.T105806.RPO44.JDHGEOM.R0OC0003   DELETED
IEF285I    VOL SER NOS= DCU1C0.
IEF285I    SYS1.UT1                              KEPT
IEF285I    VOL SER NOS= DCU1C0.
IEF285I    GOSET                                 PASSED
IEF285I    VOL SER NOS= DCU1C0.
IEF285I    SYSOUT                                SYSOUT
IEF285I    VOL SER NOS=         .
 **** TIME NOW= 10 HRS. 58 MIN. 16 SEC.   JOB= JDHGEOM   STEP= LKED    ****
IEF236I ALLOC. FOR JDHGEOM   GO
IEF237I PGM=*.DD ON 1C0
IEF237I FT05F001 ON 171
IEF237I FT07F0C1 ON 173
IEF237I FT01F001 ON 1C0
IEF237I FTC2F001 ON 291
IEF237I FT03F001 ON 292
IEF237I FT04F001 ON 292
```

Figure 6.6 (continued)

```
              GEOMETRIC SERIES                              Page 7
   BASE      NO. TERMS       SUM

   0.50         10        0.99902344
   0.50         20        0.99999905
   0.50         30        0.99999994
   0.90         30        8.61845970
   0.90         40        8.86694622
   0.90         50        8.95358467
```

```
                                                            Page 8
   IEF285I   GOSET                           PASSED
   IEF285I   VOL SER NOS= DCU1C0.
   IEF285I   SYSOUT                          SYSOUT
   IEF285I   VOL SER NOS=           .
   IEF285I   SYS1.UT1                        KEPT
   IEF285I   VOL SER NOS= DCU1C0.
   IEF285I   SYS1.UT2                        KEPT
   IEF285I   VOL SER NOS= DCU027.
   IEF285I   SYS1.UT3                        KEPT
   IEF285I   VOL SER NOS= DCU015.
   IEF285I   SYS1.UT4                        KEPT
   IEF285I   VOL SER NOS= DCU015.
   **** TIME NOW= 10 HRS. 58 MIN. 18 SEC.  JOB= JDHGEOM  STEP= GO  ****
   IEF285I   GOSET                           DELETED
   IEF285I   VOL SER NOS= DCU1C0.
```

Figure 6.6 (continued)

EXERCISE 6.5

Suppose that in the program called GEOM, you had made a keypunching error in the ninth statement, so that instead of

$$I = I + 1$$

you had punched

$$I = I * 1$$

with the rest of the program the same. What do you think would happen?

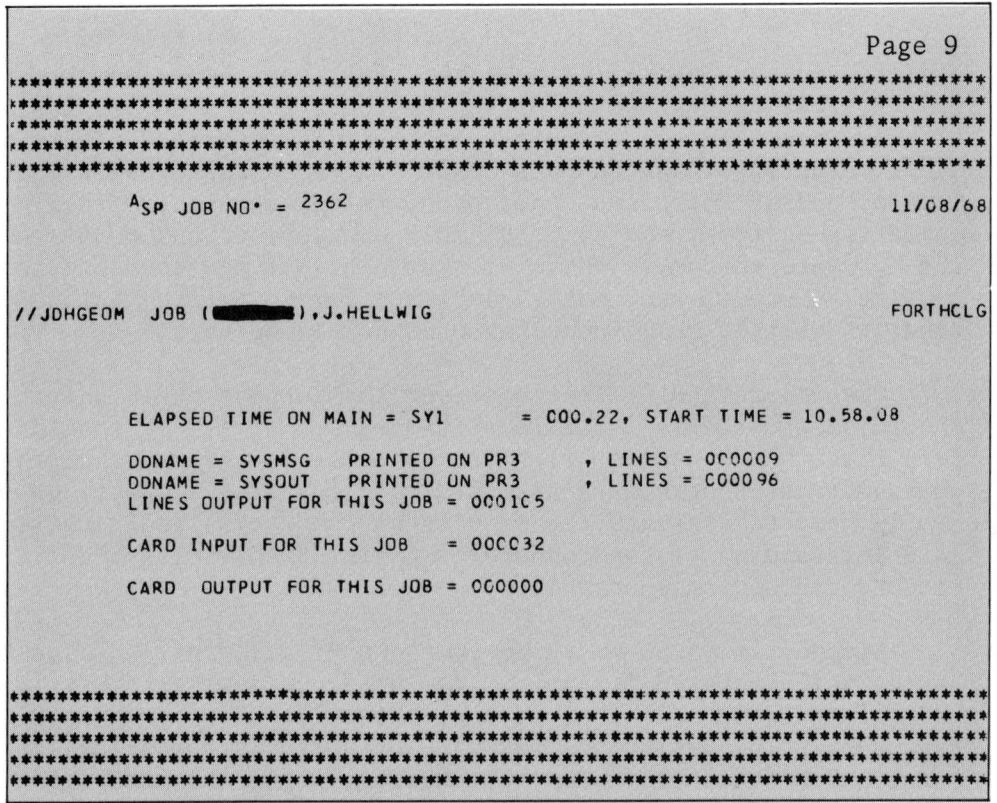

Figure 6.6 (concluded)

In particular, what job steps would be carried out? What would the output of each step look like? What system diagnostics could you expect?

This is a difficult question. Consider it carefully before you look at the answer.

Check your answer before going on.

7. *Conclusion*

If you have stayed with us this far, you should now have a fairly clear understanding of the concepts that underlie the use of high-speed digital computers as tools in research. There are other computers than the ones described here, and other computer manufacturers; there are other programming languages, other operating systems, and even entirely new generations of software and hardware to come. There will probably be new concepts in computer systems, too, but -- at least for some time -- the new concepts will be built upon the ones developed here.

The understanding that has been the purpose of this text should be of benefit in at least two ways. First, it should help those whose contact with the computer is indirect; whether you supervise programmers assigned to a research project, or simply need to evaluate the results of computer-aided research, an understanding of the computer's basic capabilities and limitations can be indispensable.

Second, if you want to do your own programming, you should now be well prepared for any of the numerous courses, texts, and reference manuals that present the rules of programming languages. In particular, FORTRAN, or a similar compiler language, should now be readily accessible, since the motivation behind many of the conventions established by programming systems have, it is hoped, been given some clarity.

APPENDIX I

THE IBM MODEL 029 KEYPUNCH

On the next page is a schematic diagram of the IBM Model 029 Keypunch. There are three parts, marked I, II, and III. Part I is much bigger in comparison to II and III than you would guess from the diagram. Parts II and III are attached to each other. They are all mounted on a small desk-type unit.

Part I is the business part of the machine; it holds, moves, and punches the cards. Part II is the control panel, and Part III is the keyboard.

Take these instructions with you to the keypunch, and follow the instructions below; the numbers in parentheses correspond to similar numbers in the diagram. After gaining some experience with using the machine, you should be able to punch up the job decks in Exercise 4.2.

Directions for Punching Cards (to be used at the keypunch)

1. Make sure the machine is on. The Power On/Power Off switch is to the right of your right knee if you're sitting at the keypunch.

2. Be sure all the switches (Part II) are in the positions illustrated in the diagram.

3. Push the Program Control Lever to the right (1), as indicated in the diagram.

4. Remove any blank cards from the Card Hopper (2).

5. Remove any blank cards in the machine by flipping up the CLEAR switch (3); the switch will automatically flip down again.

6. Remove any cards from the Card Stacker (4).

7. Push back the Sliding Pressure Plate (5), put your blank

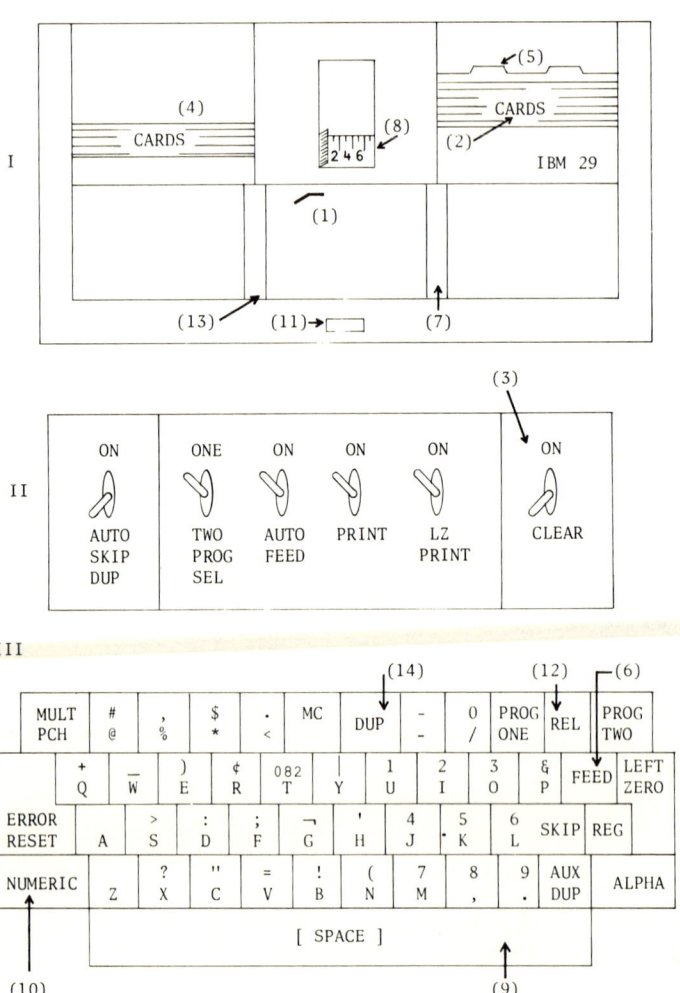

cards in the Card Hopper (2), and let the plate fall back
against the cards. Cards should be sitting face toward you,
12-edge up.

8.   Press the FEED (6) button twice. The first blank card will
drop down; then it will be positioned for punching under the
Punch Head (7) and the second card will drop down behind it.

9.   The Column Indicator (8) shows which column is about to be
punched; it should now be at column 1.

10. Punch the first card, using the keyboard like a typewriter.
You can advance to any column by using the Space Bar (9). Numbers and other 'upper case' characters - the ones stamped on the
upper part of the key - are punched by holding down the NUMERIC
key (10) while depressing the appropriate keys. You can backspace to an earlier column by pressing the Backspace Key (11).

11. When you have finished punching a card, press the RELease
key (12) to skip over the unpunched columns and bring the next
blank card into position for punching.

12. When you have finished punching all your cards, clear the
machine of cards by snapping up the CLEAR switch (3). Remove
your cards from the Card Stacker (4) and discard any blank
cards at the end of the deck. Do not leave discarded cards
lying around, as they can cause trouble for other people.

Directions for Correcting Cards

   Suppose you have punched 'V' instead of '=' in column 16.
There are two possibilities; either you notice it before you
start to punch the next card, or you do not.

A. If you notice the error before you have started punching
    the next card:

    1.   If part of the erroneous card is still under the Punch
         Head (7), hit REL (12) once. If the erroneous card
         has already been RELeased, then do not hit REL.

2. The erroneous card is now positioned at the Read Head (13), and the next blank card is ready at the Punch Head. The Column Indicator (8) should be at Column 1.

3. Hold down the DUP key (14) to reproduce the punches in the first 15 columns. (Be careful; the DUP key can run away with you.) When the column indicator is at 16, stop duplicating and punch the '='.

4. Hold down the DUP key to copy the rest of the punches on the old card.

5. When you take your deck from the Stacker after you have finished, be sure to remove the erroneous card from the deck.

B. If you notice the error after you are all through and are proofreading the deck:

1. Clear the machine (Directions for Punching Cards, Step 5).

2. Take the erroneous card and put a blank card behind it.

3. Put these two cards in front of any other cards in the Card Hopper (Directions for Punching Cards, Step 7).

4. Press FEED (6) twice; then press REL once.

5. Follow steps 2 through 4 of A, above.

6. Clear the machine.

7. Remove the two cards from the Card Stacker, throw away the bad one, and put the good one *in its place* in your deck.

APPENDIX II

ANSWERS TO EXERCISES

1.1 *Step 4.* Multiply it by R.
   Step 6. Transfer control to 3.
Note: If you said "transfer control to 1," look again and see what would happen if the program were written this way. The first term would be set equal to R (steps 1, 2), and the second term to R^2 (steps 3, 4, 5). Then if we were to transfer to 1, we would again read in a value of R, set the first term to R, and set the next term to R^2. If we transfer to 3, however, the 'term just computed' is R^2, and we set the next term to R^3 as required.

1.2 1, 2, 3, 4, 5, 6, 3, 4, 5, 6, 3, 4, etc.

1.3

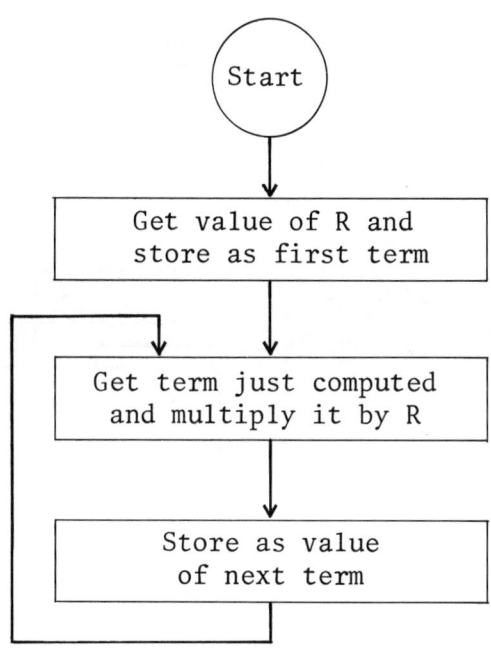

1.4 1, 1/2, 1/4, 0, 1/2, 3/4.

199

1.5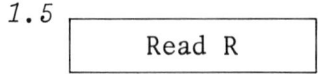

1.6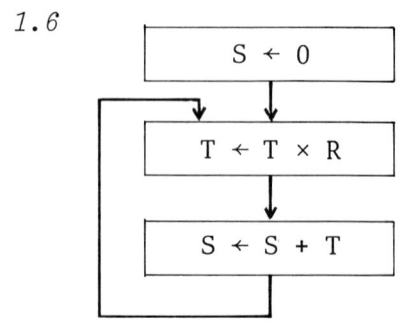

1.7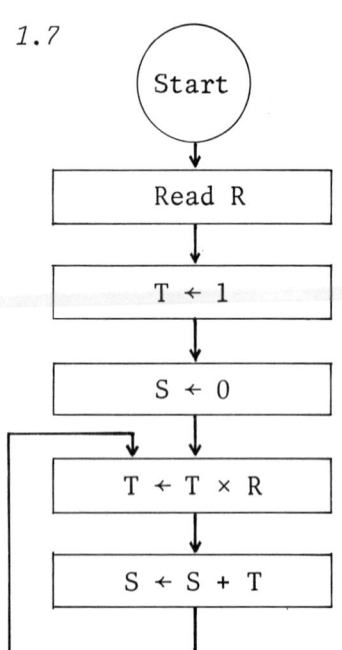

The diagram to the left is preferable; the input box could also be inserted in either of these two places:

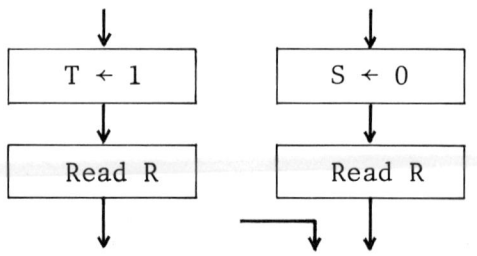

but neither of these is very good form. The following is dead wrong:

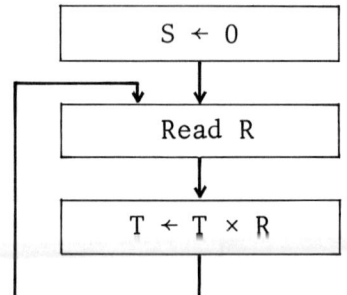

Here we would read a new value of R before computing each term of the series, whereas R is to remain the same for all terms.

1.8

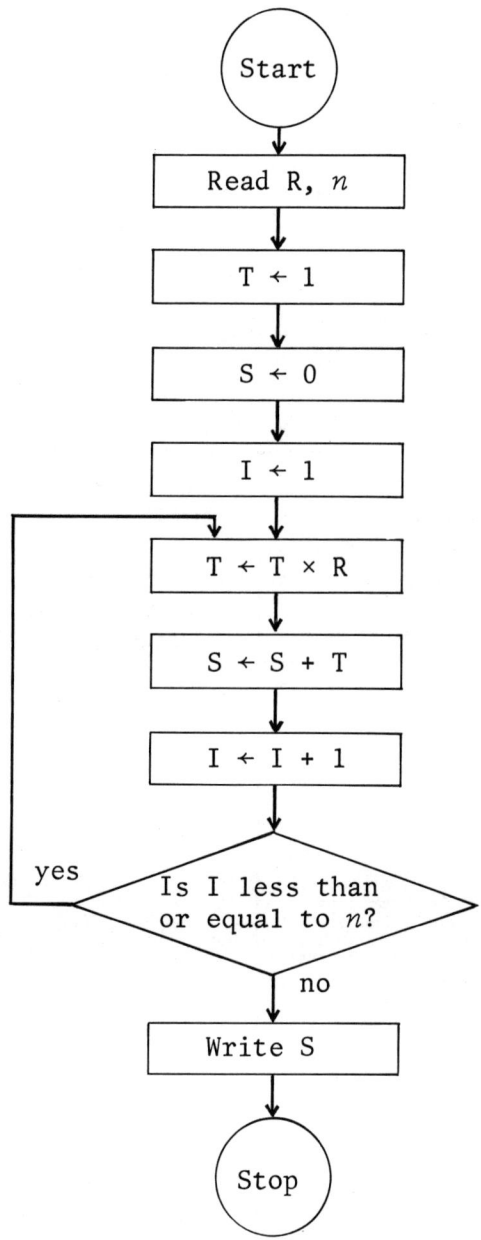

2.1

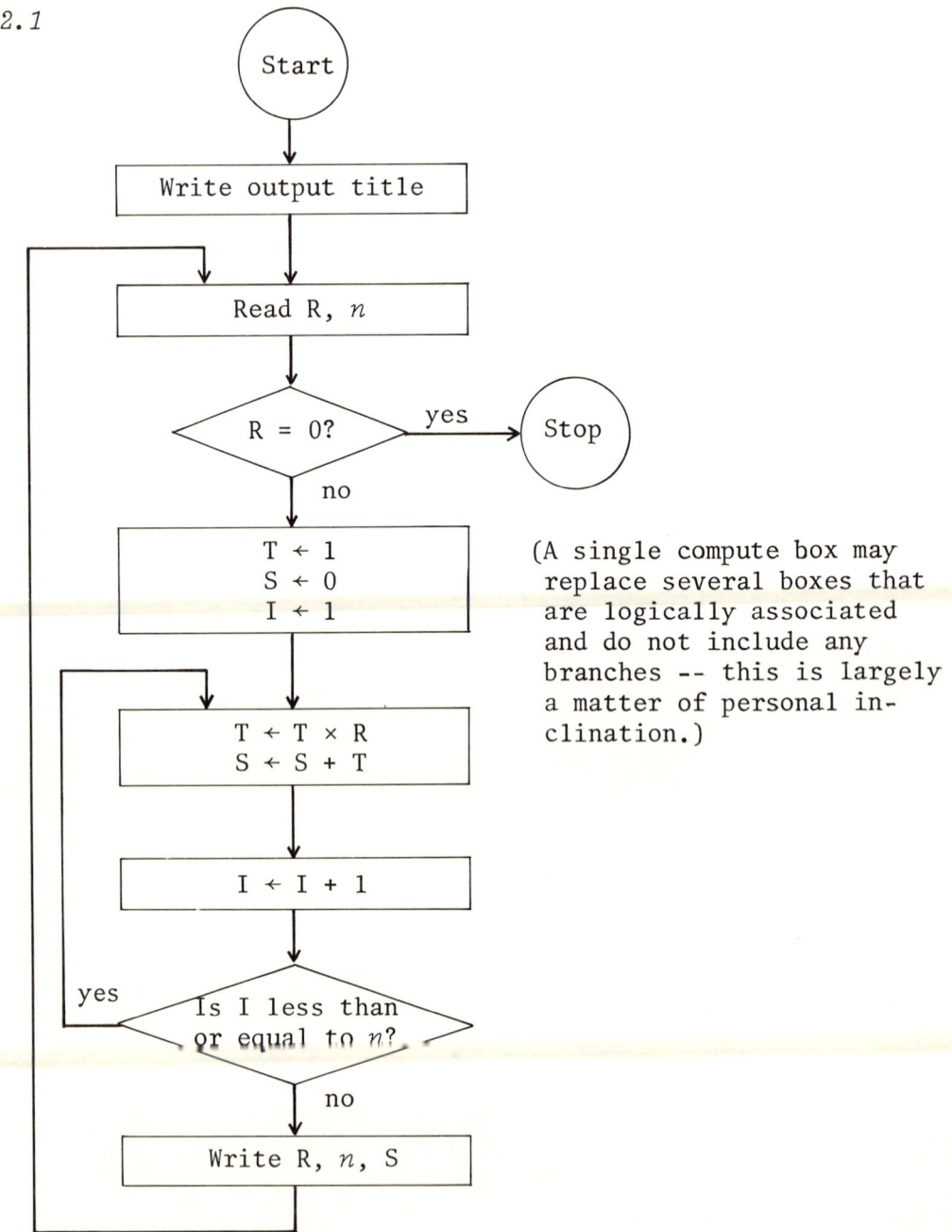

(A single compute box may replace several boxes that are logically associated and do not include any branches -- this is largely a matter of personal inclination.)

2.2
```
              PRINT 13
    2         READ 14,R,N
              IF (R .EQ. 0) STOP
              T=1
              S=0
              I=1
    7         T=T*R
              S=S+T
              I=I+1
              IF (I .LE. N) GO TO 7
              PRINT 15,R,N,S
              GO TO 2
    13        FORMAT ('1          GEOMETRIC SERIES'//
              .'   BASE    NO. TERMS      SUM'//)
    14        FORMAT (F5.2,I5)
    15        FORMAT (F7.2,I9,6X,F11.8)
              END
```

3.1

Register	Before Statement 37	After Statement 37	After 38	After 39
(CPU)	unknown	2	5	7
592	not yet defined	2	2	7
608	2	2	2	2
612	not yet defined	not yet defined	5	5
642	5	5	5	5

3.4 (a) 16

(b) In the method illustrated, only one position is ever punched at a time. More complicated codes, which allow more than one position to be punched at a time, also would allow more towns to be represented.

(c) If position 1 is punched,
   punch in position 2 : Lynn
   punch in position 3 : Swampscott
   punch in position 4 : Salem
If position 1 is not punched,
   punch in position 2 : Beverly
   punch in position 3 : Montserrat
   punch in position 4 : Prides Crossing

3.5   -7 to +7.

3.6   (a)   594.7
      (b)   3060.08

3.7   (a) $(7 \times 10^3) + (9 \times 10^1) + (2 \times 10^0)$
      (b) $(5 \times 10^2) + (6 \times 10^1) + (6 \times 10^0) + (7 \times 10^{-1})$
      (c) $(1 \times 10^{-1}) + (1 \times 10^{-2}) + (4 \times 10^{-4})$

3.9   Sixteen. We can use the ten numerals of the decimal system, but we'll need six more. Because of the way numerals are used in a positional system, they must be single characters. Let's steal six symbols from the alphabet and use them as hexadecimal numerals. The following table shows the decimal-hexadecimal correspondence for one-digit numbers:

Decimal	Hexadecimal	Decimal	Hexadecimal
0	0	8	8
1	1	9	9
2	2	10	A
3	3	11	B
4	4	12	C
5	5	13	D
6	6	14	E
7	7	15	F

3.10 $22_{16} = (2 \times 16^1) + (2 \times 16^0)$
            $= 32 + 2$
            $= 34$

      $10_{16} = (1 \times 16^1) + (0 \times 16^0)$
              $= 16$

      $109_{16} = (1 \times 16^2) + (0 \times 16^1) + (9 \times 16^0)$
               $= 256 + 0 + 9$
               $= 265$

3.11 $1F_{16} = (1 \times 16^1) + (15 \times 16^0)$
              $= 16 + 15$
              $= 31$

$$C2_{16} = (12 \times 16^1) + (2 \times 16^0)$$
$$= 192 + 2$$
$$= 194$$

$$FF_{16} = (15 \times 16^1) + (15 \times 16^0)$$
$$= 240 + 15$$
$$= 255$$

3.12   (a) 0011
        (b) 1101
        (c) 1010
        (d) 0110

3.13   (a) -7
        (b) +1
        (c) +7
        (d) -4

3.14   help

3.15   10001001   10000110

3.16   92 89 A2 A2

3.17   kiss

3.18   Principally because not all bit configurations can be represented by one of the EBCDIC characters. EBCDIC is an 8-bit code, and there are 256 different configurations of 8 bits. The standard characters used for communication -- 26 upper case letters, 26 lower, 10 numerals, and about 20 punctuation and other special characters -- don't provide representation for nearly enough 8-bit configurations. For example, the following *byte*

11100001

can be represented by the hexadecimal number E1; it corresponds to no EBCDIC character.

Thus EBCDIC allows us to represent the standard character set by an 8-bit code. But it does not, on the other hand, afford a way of representing any 8-bit binary pattern.

3.19 You can't. Only by knowing some things about the state of the computer at the time it encounters a given word can you know how it will be interpreted. If the *address* of this word appears in the 'instruction counter' (see Section 3), then the word will be treated as an instruction. If its address appears in the operand portion of an instruction that treats data as EBCDIC characters, then the word will be treated as an EBCDIC character string.

3.20 (a) If the address of the word appears as the operand of an integer arithmetic instruction, then the word will be treated as an integer. It would be a negative integer, since the left-most bit is 1. Its absolute value decimal equivalent is nearly two billion.

(b) If the address of the word appears as the operand of a floating-point arithmetic instruction, then the word will be treated as a number in floating-point (signed fraction with signed exponent) format. If the word in the exercise were treated thus, it would correspond roughly to the decimal number

$$-0.2 \times 10^{-55}$$

6.1 Look to statement 4 (D = SQRT((... etc.) which has been assigned internal statement number ISN0006. (See page 3 of the output listing in Figure 6.1.)

6.2 The instruction has byte numbers 000170 through 000173. This is deduced by the following steps:

    1. In statement 3 of the source program we ask if C is equal to zero, and nowhere else. The statement reads

        3   IF (C .EQ. 0) STOP

    2. In the object listing, page 4 of Figure 6.1, we find an entry '3' in the symbolic-address column, which corresponds to source statement number 3. The full line reads

    000170 78 00 D 068   3 LE   0, 104(0,13)   C

    3. The symbolic reference for this line is C, and there is no other reference to C in this section of code, so we must be getting C from memory to see if it is zero. (The symbolic instruction code 'LE' is 'load from memory.')

4. This instruction is given the initial number 000170, and it is four bytes long. Therefore it must have byte numbers 000170 through 000173.

6.3 The second version is wrong. What might make you suspicious is that the depth computed for the first two cases is the same, although there is a significant difference in the range, and the echo time is the same. This is not necessarily wrong. A large difference in the range could imply only a small difference in the depth; a difference of half a foot would not show up, since we are printing whole numbers in the output. Nevertheless, it is the sort of thing to make one suspicious.

In fact, the error is in statement 4, which reads, in the second version:

$$D = SQRT ((4920 * T/2)**2 - (C/2))$$

The quantity C/2 has not been squared, as it should be. As a result, the magnitude of C does not contribute enough to the equation for D, and a large change in C produces a negligible change in D.

The results printed out for both programs have been rounded. The values for D computed by the erroneous version of the program, if carried out to greater precision, are:

```
       ATALANTA - BEHEMOTH DEPTH CALCULATIONS

RANGE (FEET)        ECHO (SECONDS)        DEPTH (FEET)


   1000.                 5.00              12299.9766
   5000.                 5.00              12299.8945
   2000.                 1.28               3148.6399
```

6.4 By reference to LABEL 000012, the compiler indicates that there is some use, in the source program, of a statement number 12, but that this statement number is undefined. There is no source statement numbered 12, which is what 'undefined' implies. Where did the reference to '12' come from?

Statement 6 has been mis-coded to read

      6   GO TO 12

instead of

      6   GO TO 2

and as there is no statement 12, statement 6 cannot be compiled. This is an obvious, serious error.

If the programmer had told the system that the job should continue in the presence of errors, the compiler would have made the best of it and generated an object program. For statement 6 it would have coded a transfer to a special library subprogram that fields execution-time errors. In the GO step, when control reached statement 6, this library subprogram would be given control; it would issue a diagnostic and give itself up to the operating system control program, thus causing termination of the job.

6.5   Since there is nothing syntactically wrong with the statement, the compiler would not diagnose it as an error. It does not in any way affect the way the program and associated library programs are loaded, so the linkage editor step would also be successful, and the object program would be allowed to go into execution.

The effect of the error is to keep the value of I at 1 forever. The value of I controls the number of times the basic loop is executed. Each time through the loop, I is compared with N, the total number of terms that are to be calculated; when I becomes greater than N, the program should print results for the first set of data and go back to read a new set.

But with the error, I will never exceed N, and the test in the tenth statement

      IF (I .LE. N) GO TO 7

will always result in a transfer to statement 7. The program is now an infinite loop; control can never reach the statement that writes out R, N, and S (unless N were zero or negative).

This means there would be no results printed during the execution phase. The program would run on and on, computing terms in the series for the first input data, until one of two possible conditions developed. One is that the time limit specified on the JOB card would be exceeded. The program would be automatically terminated by the system, or manually terminated by the computer operators, and a message would be printed to this effect.

The other possibility is that before the time estimate could be exceeded, the values of S or T might become either too large or too small for the computer to handle meaningfully. (Whether they become large or small depends on whether the value of R is greater than or less than 1.) This condition is called *overflow* (number too large) or *underflow* (number too small). The computer can detect its own inability to cope with these conditions, and can take action accordingly; one action it may take is to terminate the job.

INDEX

Accounting for computer time, 114, 120, 128, 152, 153, 174-75, 179
Active program, 146, 148, 154
Address, 48, 53, 54, 206
  absolute, 174
  symbolic, 170, 171
Algorithm, 157
Allocation of resources, 167
Alphabetic information, 39, 78-80, 88-89, 206
Animated movies, 111
Application program, 74
Arithmetic operations, 2, 6, 15, 64, 72-73, 82
Arithmetic unit, 3, 5
ASP, 135-43, 144, 158, 160, 174
Assembler, 82-83
Assignment operation, 9-10, 42

Batch-processing, 121-28, 129, 130, 132, 135, 137, 143-44
Binary, 55
  see Codes
  number system, 61, 68-73
Bit, 55, 104
Blank character, 80, 94
Blocking, 132, 137
Braille, 110
Branch, 16
  see Control, transfer of
Buffer, 132, 137
Byte, 49, 55, 83-84, 94, 98, 169

Card, *see* Punched card
Card code, *see* Codes
Card image, 104, 122, 132
Card reader, 91, 97, 118, 128, 137
Card-to-tape conversion, 104, 122
Cathode-ray-tube screen, 111-12
Code conversion, 98-99
Codes,
  alphabetic, 78-80
    see also EBCDIC
  binary, 55-61, 68-73, 75-80, 82-84, 90
  card, 94, 98-99
  hexadecimal, 83-84
  Hollerith, 58, 94
  instruction, 24-27, 82-83, 169-72
Coding, program, 24, 40-43
Collating sequence, 80
Columbia University Computer Center, 1, 114, 118, 135, 142, 159
Communication among programs, 29, 127, 172-73
Compiler, *see* FORTRAN
Computation-bound job, 144-46
Control, 2-3
  flow of, 7-9, 15-18, 42, 46
  transfer of, 7, 9, 15-18, 53-54, 131
Control program (Supervisor), 132-34, 137, 139, 145-46, 179, 182
  see also Monitor program
Control statements (Control cards), 100, 114-18, 124-28, 144, 160, 182
Control unit, 3, 5, 6, 28, 49, 53-54

211

Conversation, 149-51, 154-55
Core, *see* Magnetic core
Counter, 22
CPU, 49-50, 53-54, 82, 120,
    131-33, 143-46, 147,
    153-54

Data, 49, 53-55, 87-89,
    97-98, 184
Data-set, *see* File
Debugging, 157-58, 159
Decision, logical, 16-17, 39, 40
Default conditions, 116, 168
Desk calculator, 2-4, 6
Diagnostics, 168, 179-82, 184, 187
Direct-access devices, 108, 137, 159
Disk storage device, 108
Documentation, 157-58
Drum storage device, 108
Dynamic loading, 139-40

EBCDIC, 80, 85, 86, 88, 91, 94, 98
Efficiency, 4, 68, 103, 109, 120, 128 *ff.*, 135, 145, 148, 156
End-of-file, 106-07, 124
Errors, 139, 149, 168, 176-77, 179-82, 184, 187
Executive program, 133
    see Control program
External statement number (ESN), 168-69

Fetch operation, 49-50, 54
File, 106-07, 124
Floating-point, *see* Numbers
Flow diagram, 7-9, 15-18, 24, 37-40

Flow of control, *see* Control
FORTRAN, 27
    compiler, 89-90, 97, 116-17, 121, 124, 127, 149, 160, 167-72, 179-82
    language, 27, 37, 40-43, 50, 87
    translator, 74, 78-79
    see also F. compiler
    variable, 41

General-purpose program, 35-36

Hardware, 73-75, 78, 98-99, 145, 176-77
Hexadecimal
    code, 83-84
    numbers, 67, 77, 84
Higher-level language, 27
Hollerith code, 58, 94

IBM 029 keypunch, 100, 195-98
IBM 1401 computer, 122-24, 135
IBM 360 computer, 1, 25, 48, 49, 54 *ff.*, 76-78, 80, 83-84, 94, 104, 114, 121, 135-43, 147
IBM 7094 computer, 60, 121-28, 135
Idle time, CPU, 120, 128 *ff.*
Infinite loop, *see* Loop
Information, 5, 24, 56, 84, 87 *ff.*
Information processing, 87-91
Information retrieval, 107-08
Input, 2-3, 5, 15, 41, 87 *ff.*, 110, 117-18
Input/Output (I/O)
    -bound job, 144
    channel, 130-31, 133, 140, 144, 145
    devices, 90-113, 120 *ff.*

Instruction counter, 53-54, 147
Instructions, 15, 24-27, 49, 53-54, 82-83
Integers, *see* Numbers
Interactive systems, 146-56
Internal machine language, 25-26, 82-84, 169-72
Internal statement number (ISN), 168-69
Interrupt, 131, 133, 145
Interval timer, 145, 146

Job, 87, 114-19, 121
Job step, 90, 160

Keypunch, 91, 94, 100, 110, 195-98

Language
   see FORTRAN l., Higher-level l., Internal machine l., Programming l., Symbolic machine l.
Library, *see* Programs, library
Light-pen, 111-12
Linkage editor, 127, 160, 172-74, 184
Load module, 172-74
Loader, 127
Loading, 125-27, 139-40
Location, *see* Memory l.
Logical decision, 16-17, 39, 40
Loop, 15-16, 97, 107
  infinite, 16, 18, 179

Magnetic core, 54-56, 68-69, 83
Magnetic tape, 103-07, 121-28, 129, 159
Magnitude (of numbers), 76-78

Main processor, 130, 135-42, 158, 160, 174-75
Man-machine communication, 90-91, 109-13, 148-55
Memory, 5-6, 27-29, 48-49, 54
   see also Storage
Memory location, 25, 28, 41, 49, 53-54, 83, 173-74
Memory register, *see* Register
Modular programming, 176
Monitor program, 124-28
   see also Control program
Multiprocessor system, 134-42
Multiprogramming, 132-34, 137-38, 140, 145, 146, 148, 153
Multi-step job, 90

Non-arithmetic information processing, 78-80, 88-89
Number systems,
  Arabic, 61
  base of, 64
  binary, 61, 68-73
  decimal, 61-62
  hexadecimal, 67, 77, 84
  octal, 64-66
  positional, 61-62, 64, 69
Numbers,
  conversion of, 74, 98-99
  decimal, 68
  floating-point, 75-78, 98
  integer, 56-57, 60, 62, 72-73
  real, 75-78

Object deck, 90, 125, 159, 167-68
Object listing, 169-72
Object program, *see* Programs
Off-line computer, 122
Operand, 54

Operators, computer, 118, 120
Operating system, *see* Systems
Optical character recognition, 110
OS/360, 115, 135, 167, 172, 184, 187
Output, 2-3, 5, 6, 15, 39, 87 *ff.*, 110, 122
Overlaying, 124-25, 139-40

Parity checking, 104-06
Peripheral computer, 122
Peripheral I/O devices, 135
Precision, 76
Printer, 39, 109-10
Printing, 42, 91, 109-10, 124, 138
Priorities, 133, 137, 144, 145
Procedure, 4, 7, 35-38
Processor, *see* Main p., Support p.
Production, 155, 157, 176
Program execution, 6, 7, 53, 90, 97, 117, 124, 125-28, 147, 160, 174
Program termination, 40, 41, 43, 97, 120, 127-28, 133, 138, 145, 179, 182, 187
Programming language, 24-27, 50, 54; 88, 121
Programming system, *see* Systems
Programs, 4, 6, 7-8, 27-30, 87-91
  active, 146, 148, 154
  application, 74
  control, *see* Control p.
  general-purpose, 35-36
  library, 121, 127, 172-73, 179, 184, 187
  object, 89-90, 97, 117, 125, 168-72
  source, 89, 117, 125, 168
  special-purpose, 35
  state of, 147
  stored, 6
  system, 74, 98, 121
  user, 74, 132-34
  see also Subprogram, Systems
Punched card, 91, 94-98, 107
Punched output, 158-59

Queues, 137-38, 144

Reading, 39-40, 87, 97-98, 105, 106-07, 127, 137, 151
Redundancy error, 105-06
Register,
  CPU, 49, 50, 53, 82, 147
  memory, 48-49, 50, 54, 83, 147, 169
Remote terminal, 110-12, 118, 139, 148-54
Retrieval of information, 5, 48, 107-08
Roll-out/Roll-in, 148, 154

Software, 73-75, 98-99, 112-13, 120 *ff.*, 177
  see also Systems
Source deck, 90, 117
Source program, *see* Programs
Special-purpose program, 35
State
  of binary device, 68
  of program, 147
Statement label, 53
Storage, 5
  intermediate (secondary), 91 *ff.*, 124-25, 154
  main, 125
  see also Memory

Store operation, 49-50
Subprogram (Subroutine), 29-30, 36-37, 42, 74, 87-88, 90
    see also Programs, library
Subsystem, 140-41
Supervisory program, 133
    see also Control program
Support processor, 135-42, 158, 160, 175
Symbolic machine language, 26-27, 37, 82, 170-72
Symbolic reference, 41, 48, 50, 83
System library,
    see Programs, library
System overhead, 174-75
System programs,
    see Programs, system
Systems,
  operating, 74, 120-21
  programming, 74, 120-21
  see also: ASP; Batch-processing; Control program; Multiprocessor system; Multiprogramming; OS/360; Software; Time-sharing; Time-slicing.

Tape, *see* Magnetic t.
Tape record, 106, 124, 125, 132
Tape recording density, 104
Tape unit, 103
Testing, program, 157, 176-77
Text-processing, *see* Non-arithmetic processing
Throughput, 134-35, 143
Time estimate for job, 116, 138, 179
Time-sharing, 146-56
Time-slicing, 143-46, 148, 153, 154
Transfer of control,
    see Control
Translation, 27, 74, 78-79, 82-83, 89-90, 168
Transmission of information, 109-10
Turn-around time, 134-35, 143-44, 149, 152-53, 154
Typewriter terminal, 91, 110

User program, 74, 132-34

Word, 49, 53, 55
Writing, *see* Output, Printing

QA
76.5
H458

NOV 3 1969